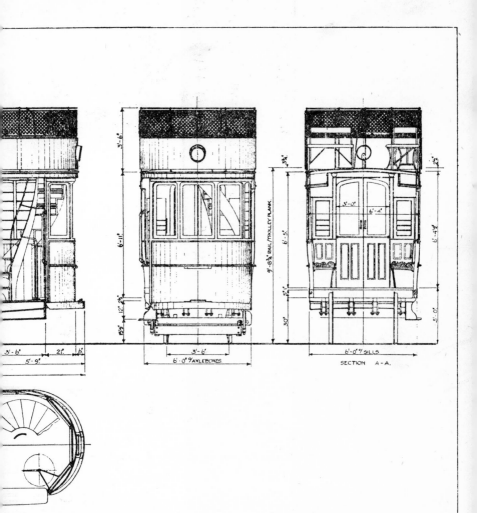

3'-6"

6'-11"

12'-2½"

15½"

3'-6"

6'-0" 9 AXLEBOXES

9'-6¾" RAIL/TROLLEY PLANK

6'-5"

5½"

5½"

5"

30"

5'-0"

6'-4½"

2'

3'-0"

6'-4"

6'-0" ½ SILLS

SECTION A-A.

3'-6"   2'1"

5'-9"

	TRUCKS:	EQUIPMENT:	BRAKES:	REMARKS:	DWG. NO.
Louis No 1900. Seating 24+29 = 53.	Builder: St Louis Car Co	Motors, 2-8"H.	Wheel, Hand.	Nos. 1-20. Interior seating later rated at 26 making total of 55, in some	
6'-6" Ht Rail/Trolley plank 9'-8¾.	Tube, Rigid No 8.	Tube, GE-58.	Electric, Rheostatic	cases. Interior finish quartered oak varnished, curtains crimson velvet stuffed.	
6'-4" Ht Rail/side, 30"	Wheelbase, 6'-0"	Rating, 27 P	Track, Special ❋ peg	This class outlasted the other three with only minor reconditioning but were given	E/099.
6'-0" Ht Rail/floor, 3'-0"	Springbase, 12'-6"	Gear ratio		accordingly. Brush Aa & Peckham P22 trucks with 6'-0" & 6'-6" wheelbase respectively.	
Ht. inside 6'4½	Wheel diam. 33"	Control BTH.		❋power type track brakes replaced the spring brakes fitted in 1903.	

THE
TRAMWAYS
OF
KENT

VOL. 2

178

The Tramways of Kent

by
"INVICTA"

Edited by G. E. BADDELEY, B.Com., M.C.I.T.

VOLUME 2 — EAST KENT

Published in London by

THE LIGHT RAILWAY TRANSPORT LEAGUE
4 Madge Hill, Church Road, Hanwell, London W7 3BW

in association with
THE TRAMWAY AND LIGHT RAILWAY SOCIETY

1975

Printed by W. J. Fowler & Son (Cricklewood) Ltd.,
Fotoscript House, Jubilee Close, Kingsbury, NW9
© G. E. Baddeley   ISBN: 0 900433 45 0

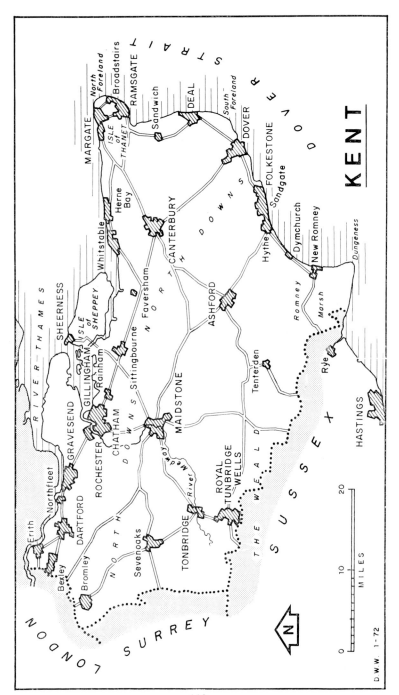

KENT

SURREY

LONDON

SUSSEX

RIVER THAMES

DOVER STRAIT

North Foreland
South Foreland

MARGATE
Broadstairs
RAMSGATE
ISLE of THANET
Sandwich
DEAL
DOVER
FOLKESTONE
Sandgate
Hythe
Dymchurch
New Romney
Dungeness

Herne Bay
Whitstable
SHEERNESS
ISLE of SHEPPEY
CANTERBURY
NORTH DOWNS
Faversham
Sittingbourne
Rainham
GILLINGHAM
CHATHAM
ROCHESTER
GRAVESEND
Northfleet
Erith
Bexley
Bromley
DARTFORD
Sevenoaks
NORTH DOWNS
MAIDSTONE
River Medway
ASHFORD
Tenterden
THE WEALD
ROYAL TUNBRIDGE WELLS
TONBRIDGE
HASTINGS
Rye
Romney Marsh

N

MILES
0   10   20

D.W.W. 1-72

180

AUTHORS' NOTE

WE have already indicated, in Volume 1, which of the authors was responsible for each chapter in both volumes. Likewise, we have named a number of kind people who have provided information used in both volumes. However, since Volume I went to press, several other people have come forward with further information of value suitable for incorporation in Volume 2. Therefore we take this opportunity of naming and expressing our thanks to them. They are Messrs. I. Gotheridge, Major Phillip Gratwicke, for the use of his father's drawings, Charles E. Lee, Eric Harrison and W. A. Camwell, for placing the results of their latest researches into the Hythe and Sandgate tramway and cliff railways at our disposal, Donald Mackenzie who gave a talk to the London Area of the Light Railway Transport League about surface contact systems, including reference to the proposals at Folkestone, Ray Warner for photographs and information on Dover tramways and to J. S. Webb & R. P. Lawson for further information on secondhand trams at Dover.

The author of the section on Herne Bay Pier Tramway wishes to express his thanks to Mr. H. E. Gough, Hon. Curator of the Herne Bay Records Society, also to R. S. Bamford, G. B. Claydon Ll.B., The Electric Power Storage Co. Ltd., C. J. Henley, J. W. Jordan, J. H. Meredith, J. H. Price, Arthur G. Wells and L. Wilding.

R H. Hiscock, Chairman of the Gravesend Historical Society, J. H. Price, S. L. Harris and J. F. Parke of the Omnibus Society have between them provided some important additional information about transport in Gravesend, Chatham and Sheerness, which have been incorporated into an Appendix at the end of this volume. A list of Tramways Managers and their dates in office, largely drawn from information supplied by J. C. Gillham, have been made into another appendix and a Thanet Company's bus fleet list supplied by the Omnibus Society makes a third appendix. Finally, as in Volume 1 there is a bibliography of all works consulted, set out in the form of an appendix. We hope that the authors of these works will accept this as our thanks to them.

---

74. Frontispiece—Tram and shipping in close proximity at Dover. Ex-Birmingham Corporation No. 22 at the "George" Corner and the newly launched "Shepperton Ferry".   Courtesy Fox Photos Ltd.

75. Opposite—The general map of Kent, repeated for the benefit of readers of this volume.   D. W. Willoughby.

Once again we must thank Mr. John Fowler and his staff together with the engravers for their patient work in making the production of this book possible. We must also make the usual apology to any author whose works we have inadvertently quoted without his permission, and to the owner of any photograph not properly acknowledged. Unfortunately other commitments have prevented D. W. Willoughby from drawing the maps and plans for this volume, but after some delays, E. Beddard has been persuaded to make them at short notice, for which he has our sincere thanks. (Mr. Willoughby did undertake some additional research on the Thanet system before relinquishing the task).

The additional time made available for the production of this volume has not been wasted. Further research has been undertaken and in particular, at the suggestion of J. V. Horn, the original author of the book on Dover Tramways, we have approached G. H. Blackburn, now on the spot and with access to certain information not formerly available, to carry out further research there, especially into the finances of the tramway undertaking, the mysterious top cover fitted for a short time to car No. 14 and further into the details of the purchase of second-hand cars in later years. The information thus obtained has been incorporated into Chapter 7, the financial details being in the form of a separate note.

We have also had more time for the detailed examination of the works of four well known transport photographers, who knew the Dover and Thanet systems well and captured with their cameras, some of the more elusive operating features and cars on these systems. They are Dr. Hugh Nicol, D. W. K. Jones, C. Carter and N. D. W. Elston, without whose reminiscenes and loan of rare photographs, this book would have been very much the poorer. (Unfortunately, after the above was written, we learned that Dr. Nicol had died and we must now tender our thanks to his executors for their kind co-operation and permitting us to continue to use his material).

The chapter and page numbers used in this volume follow on from those in Volume 1. This is done to emphasise the continuity of the subject matter, but also for the benefit of readers and to save them from having to keep referring to volume 1, we have repeated the general map of Kent at the beginning of the book.

Once again, we shall be very pleased to receive any corrections sent in by readers and will publish them as set out in the Authors' Note to Volume 1.

"Invicta"	Geoffrey Baddeley,	Albert McCall,
	Winstan Bond,	John Price,
	Robert Brimblecombe,	David Scotney,
	Anthony Graham,	George Stevens,
Croydon 1975.	Richard Elliott,	David Willoughby.

INTRODUCTION TO VOLUME 2

THIS introduction will be short, as most of the things that have to be said, have already been said in the Introduction to Volume 1.

This volume deals with the history of the tramways on the Kent coast, which started out with very rosy prospects of serving rapidly developing seaside resorts and which it was said would soon make a continuous chain round that coast. There is no doubt that for many years, in spite of its early history being tarnished by a number of spectacular accidents, once the accident-prone cars had been rebuilt, the Thanet undertaking did reap a considerable harvest from holiday traffic and later gained a reputation for good service to the public. Ironically, its demise was eventually brought about by pressure being brought to bear on the Company's other activities.

Dover is best known as a Channel Port, but does have a seaside area with a lengthy promenade. However its tramway system, which was notable for being the first electric tramway in the South of England, did not really serve the seaside area, but comprised two routes running inland along the main roads leading to Canterbury and Folkestone; they also served the docks. The Kent coast suffered badly from bombardment and wholesale evacuation of the population during the 1914-1918 war; both the Thanet system and Dover were the victims of actual material damage and very heavy loss of traffic, so that in the early 1920s they had a hard struggle to rehabilitate their undertakings, on which both cars and track were then in a run-down state.

Thanet embarked on a systematic and extensive rebuilding programme, while Dover went into the second-hand market, in order to renew most of its time-worn fleet. Your editor well remembers that while attending a cadet camp at Shorncliffe in 1935, he visited Dover. Having been told that Dover had a fleet of nice little green open top cars, on coming over the hill at Maxton, he was surprised to see a squat covered top car in a dull brown livery (Car No. 8) waiting at the terminus. A few minutes later, our bus passed a taller covered top car (No. 19) on Priory Station bridge and this appeared to be in a black and cream livery. Indeed, by the end of the day, having seen cars of several designs, painted in blue, brown, red and green liveries, he was convinced that Dover had no two cars alike nor in the same livery!

The wayward Hythe & Sandgate horse (and mule) tramway, although originally a feeder to a railway, later became a pawn in much wider plans in the Folkestone area. These foundered after several brave attempts and in effect by delaying its electrification while they argued with the authorities, eventually brought down the Sandgate line as well.

In this volume, we also cover the several interesting sidelines such as cliff railways, pier tramways and the Ramsgate Tunnel Railway, which complete the pattern of railed transport provided in the towns under examination. To maintain the standard of coverage set in volume 1, we have also described the extensive feeder bus services provided by the Thanet Company, even though its fleet details were rather complicated and are given as an Appendix.

In the chapter on Proposed Tramways, we have sought out information on the various elements which would have made up the true networks of interurban tramways in the County of Kent, had a little more energy been shown and the hand of the law weighed less heavily upon them.

May the readers share the fascination that we have found in tracing the history of this very interesting facet in the development of transport and urbanization in the South East of England.

Geoffrey E. Baddeley

Croydon 1975

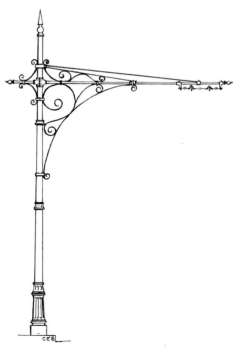

CONTENTS

END PAPERS
Isle of Thanet St. Louis single truck car in original condition.
           Drawn by late Walter Gratwicke Front
Dover Corporation No. 15 in original condition.
           Drawn by Peter Hamond Rear

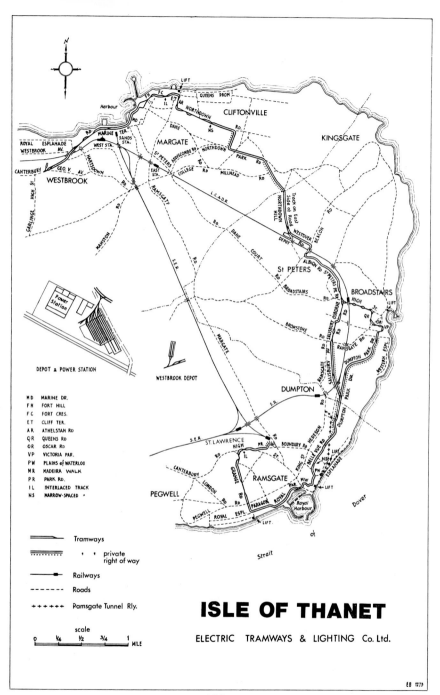

ISLE OF THANET

ELECTRIC TRAMWAYS & LIGHTING Co. Ltd.

EB 1279

186

CHAPTER FIVE

THE ISLE OF THANET ELECTRIC TRAMWAYS & LIGHTING CO. LTD.

THANET is an island in the North Sea off the north-east corner of Kent.

In ancient times, as much an island as the Isle of Wight, it is now separated from the mainland by only a few feet of water which passes unnoticed as one travels from the west but which causes a mediaeval style interruption coming over the Stour when one passes over the toll bridge at Sandwich. In the Middle Ages, a bastion against seaborne attack, in later times a source of corn and fish and all the while conducting a respectable seaborne trade with London and the Continent, the island became in the 19th and 20th centuries a place familiar to people of Southern England, who came to enjoy the even climate and clean air. Margate, Broadstairs and Ramsgate were not only holiday resorts, but a natural site for schools and hospitals.

People came by sea from London and later by rail as well, either by the London Chatham & Dover Railway, which arriving at Margate, took them round the island to Broadstairs and down through a tunnel to a station on Ramsgate Harbour. This line was opened in October 1863 and closed on 2nd July 1926; there is now an amusement park on the site of the Ramsgate Station. Alternatively they came by the South Eastern Railway to the old Ramsgate Town Station, opened on 13th April 1847 (east of the present station) from whence a branch line crossed the island to Margate Sands Station, opened on 1st December 1847, next to the Hall by the Sea (now Dreamland Amusement Park and orginally intended for yet another station.) Both stations were close to the sea front.

---

76. Opposite—Track layout map of the Thanet tramway system.
E. Beddard.

77. Above—The badge of the Thanet Company, comprising the coats of arms of Margate, Broadstairs and Ramsgate.
Drawn by G. E. Baddeley.

From this description it is easy to understand the feelings of nostalgia aroused by the tramways, which served the three towns. Local people might remember their shortcomings — "They're even in the Bible, 'the Lord made all creeping things'", "One of them almost demolished the Town Hall." But for many more, they are associated with hot summer days and a ride on the open top deck in sight of the sea, and the pitching of the cars, top-heavy with holidaymakers, the cloud of dust on the reserved track sections and the occasional stops for dewirement ("Shove it back someone up there will you?") were all part of the fun. Even locals will rhapsodise about the sight of a tram crossing the cornfields between Cliftonville and St Peter's, or about the Sunday School outings in specially hired cars.

Early Projects 1871-1887

The early proposals might, had they been practicable, have linked Margate not only with Birchington and Sandwich but with Deal, Dover and even Brighton. These were the days of rough roads when rail transport offered faster, smoother travel even when the motive power was a horse. So in 1871 the Dover, Deal, Sandwich and Ramsgate Tramway Co. applied for permission to build a line 21 miles, 24 Chains long, 4ft 8½in gauge from Beach Street Dover to Ramsgate Town Station. Initial opposition from the Turnpike Trustees was overcome, but in an excess of enthusiasm the company reported to the Board of Trade that the Trustees supported the proposal when in fact they only went so far as not to oppose it. Consent was refused, to show the Board's disapproval of the irregularity.

In the following year the Kent Tramways Co. tried again for a more ambitious plan comprising 29 miles 48 chains of route, with a branch line in Dover and an extension to Margate along the turnpike road, finishing at the Shakespeare public house on Margate sea front after running along Eaton Road. An Act was passed in 1873, but no work was done, presumably through lack of money. This was not the last attempt, for in 1899 the Cinque Ports Light Railway proposed linking Ramsgate, Dover and Hastings (see Chapter 8) and in 1904 mention was made in the "Light Railway & Tramway Journal" of a plan to connect tramways in Brighton and places further west with the existing tramways on the Isle of Thanet.

Less ambitious plans on the Isle of Thanet itself were slightly more successful. The Ramsgate and Margate Tramways Act of 1879 allowed the building of a 2 foot 6½ inch gauge line, 6 miles 35 chains long, out of the 6 miles 65 chains asked for, by which horse-drawn trams would have gone from Ramsgate to Margate by way of St. Peters. The following year saw another Act in which the Company was allowed to use steam power and in further powers granted in 1882, the gauge allowed was widened to 3 feet 6 inches. A mile of

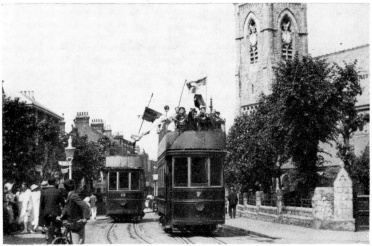

Early views in Margate.

78. Above—The sea front at Margate with No. 47 near the Station with a six window vestibule and 57 with its original two window semi-vestibule.   Pamlin Prints.

79. Below—Car No. 7 with a Sunday School outing, passing the church in Northdown Road, Cliftonville.
No. 7 is just running onto a section where the two tracks were too close together for cars to pass.   C. Carter.

track was actually constructed, from St. Peter's Church to Broadstairs Railway Station, passing along High Street and St. Peter's Road, but the opposition from Margate and Ramsgate Councils and frequent changes of plan by the Company meant that the line was never completed. "Keble's Gazette" gave the tone of the discussions in reporting a meeting of Margate Council in January 1884: "Mr. Johnstone then proceeded to give the distances which it was proposed to have between the tram lines and the kerb, where the lines were double, showing that in some instances a distance of five inches and a half would not intervene, and that in others the distance would be but two inches and a half, and he said that in these instances ladies would be unable to pass, especially in the now fashionable dresses, which trailed about two feet behind them!!" By 1884, the Company's resources were exhausted and although a meeting of the property-owners and rate-payers expressed their support and the local authorities seemed to be about to come out in favour of the company, it was wound up and its resources sold to pay the creditors.

If a report of a photograph of a horse car at St. Peters is to be believed, the car may actually have been delivered, but cannot have remained there long. Certainly £301 was spent on "cars" which in those days would have been about the price of one car. However, when a horse tram service was inaugurated at South Shields on 10th November 1882, one of the cars was said to have been intended for the Isle of Thanet. Recent research shows that it must have been one of the cars subsequently sold to Douglas in the Isle of Man in March 1887. These were six in number and became Nos. 13-18 at Douglas. No. 18 was the odd one which differed from the others and therefore presumably the ex-Thanet car. If so, remarkably, it is still in existence as No. 18 was later rebuilt as a single decker and is retained as a "bad weather" car.

Yet other plans came to nothing. In 1880, a 3 miles 5 chains horse powered line was projected from Ramsgate to Pegwell Bay, but neither this nor the proposals of 1886 and 1887 for a line along the sea front from Margate the "Hoy" to the "Dog & Duck", Westbrook were sanctioned. However, a Bill was presented to Parliament in 1888 for the following tramways in Margate:—

Tramway No. 1 — 4 furlongs, 0.8 chains all double track.
Commencing in the "Parade" Margate 30 feet from the south-west corner of Paradise Street, to the Marine Terrace, Canterbury Road by the entrance to the London, Chatham and Dover Railway Station.

Tramway No. 2 — 2 furlongs, 6 chains single line and 6 chains double line.

Commencing at the termination of Tramway No. 1, continuing along Canterbury Road to 35 feet east of No. 19 Canterbury Road, Westbrook.

The gauge was to be 3 feet 6 inches and the capital £30,000. Horse or electric traction could be used. Not a very ambitious scheme, nevertheless it does not appear to have been sanctioned. So far the problems appear to have been caused by careless planning and the need to get approval from each of the local authorities whose area was traversed, each with its own demands to make about road widening and other matters. The Companies Department of the Board of Trade states the Ramsgate & Margate Tramways Co. Ltd. was dissolved by an order of the High Court on 1st August 1893. However, in August 1896, the situation was changed by the passing of the Light Railways Act.

The Light Railways Act and William Martin Murphy.

The Act was really intended to relieve agricultural depression and bring the producer and the consumer closer together, by facilitating railway construction in remote districts and encouraging branch lines and feeders to existing railways. In the event, it was much used to promote lines that were practically tramways, especially where there was already a railway in existence, because a tramway which joined two or more authorities could take advantage of it. So, on 3rd November 1896, Mr. William Martin Murphy promoted the Isle of Thanet Light Railways (Electric) Company Limited, with a capital of £1,000, underwritten by the Bank of Ireland and the Capital & Counties Bank and applied for a Light Railways Order. The line was initially planned to run from Pegwell Bay, through Ramsgate to Westgate. This comprised 11½ miles of 3 ft. 6 in. gauge electric tramway.

Mr. Murphy was the son of a Bantry building contractor who took over his father's business at the age of 19 and in 1878 became a director of the Central Tramways Co., of Dublin. Becoming interested in electric traction, he visited the United States in 1895 with a deputation from the Dublin United Tramways Company, including Mr. H. F. Parshall, who was to be the consulting engineer for the Thanet undertaking. He took a leading part in the construction of tramways, not only there but also in Dublin, Belfast, Cork, London Southern, Hastings, Bournemouth, Poole and Paisley as well as railways in Ireland and on the Gold Coast. Mr. Murphy eventually became Chairman of the Dublin United Tramways.

An inquiry was held at Ramsgate on 10th May 1897 and the application was approved with the exception of the line to Pegwell Bay, but unfortunately the application to Parliament did not include the section through from Margate to Westgate, a fact which Mr. Murphy must have regretted later, for permission was not then forthcoming.

The Light Railways Order applied for in 1896, under the Act of that year, made provision for the following sections of line:—

Railway No. 1. — Not approved.
(this was to have connected Pegwell Road (Cliffs' End) with Grange Road at St. Augustine's Road, Ramsgate).

Railway No. 2. — Length 4.60 chains.
Westcliffe New Approach Road to Royal Hotel, Ramsgate.

Railway No. 3. — Length 6.00 chains.
From the Royal Hotel at the junction of York Street and Military Road along Military Road.

Railway No. 4. — Length 1 furlong 2.50 chains.
From the Royal Hotel along Harbour Street to Ramsgate Harbour Station (London, Chatham & Dover Railway).

Railway No. 5. — Length 4 furlongs 5.70 chains.
From the Royal Hotel along Harbour Street, Madiera Road (sic), Wellington Crescent, Plain of Waterloo (sic), Bellevue Road to Arklow Terrace.

Railway No. 6. — Length 4 furlongs 9.35 chains.
Commencing at the termination of Railway No. 5, crossing Thanet Road and across fields past the north-east corner of Judith College to a field owned by the executors of R. Croft, 8 chains south of the northern entrance of the Broadstairs-Ramsgate Harbour railway tunnel.

Railway No. 7. — Length 6 furlongs 6.10 chains.
Commencing at the termination of Railway No. 6 and across fields belonging to the Yarrow Trustees to a point 40 chains north of the junction with Victory Road. (sic) (now Victoria Parade).

Railway No. 8. — Length 6 furlongs.
A continuation of Railway No. 7 along Victory Avenue, Granville Road Victory Avenue, Oscar Road, Broadstairs and through property belonging to William Alexander MacKinnon & Julian Arnold, into Queens Road, High Street and St. Peter's Road to St. Peter's Park Road two chains north of its junction with St. Peter's Road.

Ramsgate in the early days.

80. Above—Bogie car No. 23 descending Madeira Walk, Ramsgate. A very early view with the destinations shown on paper window slips. Note waterfall on left. Courtesy J. H. Price.

81. Below—A slightly later view of Ramsgate Harbour, showing Nos. 8 & 21 passing on the main line, with No. 45 on the spur. By now, black metal route plates were in use to indicate destinations. Courtesy J. H. Price

Railway No. 9. — Length 1 mile 0 furlongs 5.45 chains.
Commencing at a junction with Railway No. 6 and crossing land belonging to the executors of R. Croft and of Lands Allotment Co., crossing Ramsgate Road into Gladstone Road, across more land belonging to the Lands Allotment Co., across Vale Road and through property belonging to Edward Stephen Goodson, along Osborne Road, across St. Peter's Road and through property of the executors of James Alexander to join Railway No. 8.

Railway No. 10. — Length 2 miles 5 furlongs 7.92 chains.
Commencing at the junction of Railways 8 & 9 and continuing along St. Peter's Park Road, Sowell Street, Albion Road, Church Street and over the bridge of the L.C. & D. Railway onto land belonging to the Ecclesiastical Commissioners and land belonging to James Taddy Friend, to near the "Wheatsheaf" public house then along (Lower) Northdown Road for 36 chains and through land belonging to Kent & Canterbury Hospital to Northdown Road at its junction with Harold Road.

Railway No. 11. — Length 7 furlongs 6.40 chains.
Commencing at the termination of Railway No. 10 and continuing along Northdown Road, Alexandra Road, Athelstan Road, Ethelbert Terrace, Cliff Terrace, Fort Crescent & Fort Hill to the junction of Fort Hill and Fort Road.

Railway No. 12. — Length 7.90 chains single track.
Commencing at the junction of Fort Hill and Fort Road and proceeding along Paradise Street to the junction of the Parade and King Street.

Railway No. 13. — Length 9.50 chains single track.
Commencing at the junction of Fort Hill and Fort Road and continuing along Fort Road to the junction of King Street and the Parade where it rejoined Railway No. 12.

Railway No. 14. — Length 3 furlongs 7.05 chains.
Commencing at the junction of Railways Nos. 12 & 13 and continuing along the Marine Drive, Marine Terrace to its junction with the approach road to Margate L.C. & D. Railway Station.

Railway No. 15. — Length 3 furlongs 4.50 chains.
A continuation of Railway No. 14 along Marine Terrace and Canterbury Road to a point 11.70 chains south-west of the junction between Westbrook Road and Canterbury Road.

Unlike a Tramways Act, a Light Railway Order did not have to quote whether single or double track was to be used in each case, but several conditions were attached to this Order. In roads of a width of 22 feet or less, interlaced track was to be laid, certain roads were to be widened for Railways 2, 3, 4 and 5, while Railway No. 4 was only to be built with the consent of Ramsgate Corporation. Railway No. 3 was to be the siding at Ramsgate Harbour for goods only. Railways Nos. 6 & 7 were to be constructed as 60 ft. wide roads. Railway No. 9 was to be constructed before Nos. 7 & 8. Railway No. 10 would be single track over the railway bridge. Railways Nos. 12 & 13 were for one way working in opposite directions.

When the Order was under consideration, Ramsgate Council asked that a Clause be included, stipulating that no part of the through route should be discontinued unless the whole were discontinued. The Order was confirmed by the Light Railway Commissioners in December 1897 and submitted to the Board of Trade on 31st January 1898. The latter confirmed it on 13th August, for 8¾ miles of route at an estimated cost of £67,595. The various Local Authorities through whose areas the line passed, had the power of compulsory acquisition after 42 years.

It may seem strange reading today, but provision was made for the carriage of cattle, dogs and sheep, which presumably would have been carried in trailers to the passenger cars. It was also suggested that the Councils might have the use of the line at night to run special vehicles for sanitary purposes. It was stipulated that no vehicle was to be wider than 6 ft. 6 in.

Very soon the Company applied for powers to extend the line at both ends and to construct loop lines in Margate and Ramsgate; an application was made for a further Order on 16th November 1898 as follows:—

Railway No. 1 — Length 1 mile 5 furlongs 2.70 chains.
Commencing in a field next to the South Eastern Railway Station (Ramsgate Town) and continuing along Ellington Park Road, Grange Road and St. Augustine's Road to the Paragon where it would join Railway No. 2 of the 1896 Order.

Railway No. 2 — Length 2 furlongs 2 chains.
A loop line from the Plains of Waterloo at its junction with Wellington Crescent, along Augusta

195

| | | Road to rejoin Railway No. 5 of the 1896 Order in Bellevue Road, Ramsgate. |

Railway No. 3 — Length 1 furlong 7.90 chains.

A loop line from Northdown Road, Margate at its junction with Dalby Road along Dalby Road, Dalby Square and Ethelbert Crescent to rejoin Railway No. 11 of the 1896 Order at the junction of Athelstan Road.

Railway No. 4 — Length 4 furlongs.

An extension of Railway No. 15 of the 1896 Order along Canterbury Road.

Railway No. 5 — Length 4 furlongs 8.50 chains.

A continuation of Railway No. 4 along Canterbury Road to the Grove, Westgate.

Railway No. 6 — Length 1 mile 5 furlongs 0.50 chains.

A continuation of Railway No. 5 along Canterbury Road from the Grove, Westgate to the Square, Birchington.

Railway No. 7 — Length 2 furlongs 4 chains.

Continuing from the Square, Birchington along Birchington High Street (sic) (Station Road) to Minnis Road outside Birchington Station. There was also to be a short siding at Birchington Square.

Objections to the scheme were heard at Westgate in Public Inquiries held on 27th March and 5th May 1899 as a result of which the lines in Westgate and Birchington i.e. Railways Nos. 5, 6 and 7 were refused, while the loop lines were refused because of objections from frontagers and the narrowness of the roads to be traversed.

What little was left was approved on 23rd February under the Isle of Thanet Light Railways (Extension) Order 1900, comprising about 2 miles of route. Two years were allowed to complete the work and a deposit of £500 was demanded. The Railways approved were Nos. 1 and 4, namely from Ramsgate Harbour to the Ramsgate Town Station and a short extension at the Margate end to the Westgate boundary at Westbrook.

The local councils concerned did not extract any wayleaves from the Company, but did require them to undertake extensive roadworks, including over three miles of new roads. These extensive new roadways are of particular interest, since although throughout the life of the trams, they were regarded as tramways on private right of way, they were in fact named and built with the intention of converting them to public roads as soon as sufficient housing development appeared along them. They formed very useful short cuts for the trams between the towns served and were paved with stone setts against the rails, but in case the driver of any other vehicle should mistake them for public roads in their then existing state, there were boards at each end proclaiming "This is a private road for the use of Tramcars only."

The Company was required by the Order of 1898 to build the line in two years and to widen the bridge under Broadstairs Station. The use of trailer cars was not permitted for passenger carrying and the spur line at Ramsgate Harbour was to be used for goods — presumably mainly for the offloading of coal for use at the power station — and not as a passenger vehicle stand. In the event, trailers were not used even for goods, but the Harbour line did provide a useful stand for short workings and coal supplies arrived direct by rail, by way of a special siding laid into the power station premises. Fares were fixed at 1d per mile with a maximum of 6d.

Meanwhile in 1896, the Company obtained powers for electric lighting in Margate and changed its title on 11th May 1899 to "Isle of Thanet Electric Tramways & Lighting Co. Ltd.," and the capital was increased to £250,000. Also in 1899, it obtained powers to supply lighting in Broadstairs and in 1901 in the Thanet Rural District, but in the end another company supplied Ramsgate; nevertheless, the electric lighting aspect was destined to play an increasingly important role in the Company's affairs. At the same time, Mr. Murphy formed the Thanet Construction Company Ltd., to build the tramway and the electric light systems, at a cost of £450,000. Kincaid, Waller and Manville were the consulting engineers.

Construction

By May 1899, the construction of the tramway system was well under way. A year later, "Railway News" wrote enthusiastically that "The time was not far distant when the coast from say, Birchington to Pegwell Bay would be one continual series of terraces, with a parade or sea drive for the whole distance" and foresaw districts at present too distant from a railway station for development, "but which with a frequent electric tramway service, will soon be covered with houses." However, by the end of 1900, work was well behind schedule and the Company had to ask for an extension of time, blaming the railway company for delays in widening the bridge at Broadstairs and certain other works. Margate Council agreed to the extension of time, on being assured that by using the "Top Road" trams could still travel the whole distance and asked that trams should start on 1st March. An Extension Order was granted on 7th June 1901.

The first 40 cars to be delivered came from the St. Louis Car Co. of America. The contract was placed on 18th December 1899 and one of them was shown at the Tramways and Light Railways Exhibition in London in June 1900, by Messrs. R. W. Blackwell & Co.

their British agents. Cars Nos. 1-20 were of an attractive design and on single trucks which were of a heavy steel type. The staircases were reversed and this feature remained standard on all Thanet cars. Nos. 21-40 were more unusual, being bogie cars 32 ft. 6 in. long, with six side windows; their distinctive feature was that the maxmium traction trucks were arranged with the pony wheels leading. The bogie cars weighed 12 tons and the four wheelers weighed 8 tons. (See Rolling Stock section for full details).

The total cost of the line was said to be not far short of £350,000. Of the 10 miles 67 chains of 3 ft. 6 in. gauge route then built, 9 miles 67 chains were double track and one mile single track making a single track mileage of 20.67 in all. The rails were of girder type, 83 lbs. to the yard, supplied in 30 foot lengths mostly by Lorain Steel Co. Fishplates of the usual pattern (24″ x 5″ x ¾″) weighed 56 lbs. per pair and were secured with six Ibbotson's bolts and lock nuts of Helicoid type. Rails were held to gauge by 2 in. x ⅜ in tie rods placed at intervals of 7 ft. 6 in. and secured with two nuts at each end. Later 83 lb. Phönix and Krupp rails were used.

On the sections between towns the line was paved with Jarrah wood blocks on a foundation of 6 in Portland cement concrete which extended 18 inches outside the rails. "Comparatively novel" said Tramway & Railway World, "is the use of macadam between the rails, which are flanked on each side with a toothed row of granite sets (sic). Where this form of construction was used, a continuous concrete sleeper 1 ft. 9 in. wide and 6 in. thick formed the foundation of the rails. All points were supplied by Askham Bros. & Wilson of Sheffield and were of crucible cast steel. Rails were bonded with 36 in lengths of 0000 B & S wire, bonds being double and of the "Crown", "Neptune" and "Chicago" types.

Power Supply and Depots

Standards were placed at 40 yard intervals and made in three sections, with a length of 30 ft. and a weight of 990 lb. each, being made by the National Tube Co. Brackets varied in length from 5 to 6 feet for centre poles and from 16 to 23 feet for side poles. Pole brackets and arms as well as some of the wrought iron work for the generating station were supplied by Messrs. J. & C. McGloughlin of Dublin. Cast iron bases for the poles came from Messrs. Kess & Walpole of Dublin. Centre poles were only to be found on street track sections along the Parade at Margate. Trolley wires were double throughout with wire suspended over the centre of each track. The wire of hard drawn copper No. "0" Gauge, had a conductivity of 98% pure copper and a breaking strain of 4,500 lbs. Section boxes were located at half mile intervals and each had a pair of continuous current feeders 0.2 inches in section, up to about half a mile from each terminus. High pressure three-core cable also ran from the main power station to Margate and Ramsgate. There were two cables in each direction with copper 0.05 sq. inch section, also telephone and test wires running underground. All cables were supplied by the British Insulated Wire Co. and laid on the solid system.

The power station was at St. Peters and a siding connected it with the London Chatham and Dover Railway line, for the reception of materials and coal. (The track laid on the quayside at Ramsgate Harbour was intended to be available for this purpose, but there is no evidence that it was ever so used.) Two sub-stations were built (not quite in time for the opening), one in Margate and the other in Ramsgate, partly in the hope of extending the line and partly for lighting purposes in Margate. In the generating station, two 200 k.w. direct-connected current tramway generators and two 300 k.w. direct-connected three phase B.T-H. generators provided power during the daytime, with a secondary battery for lighting in Broadstairs. The motive power was provided by two engines built by E. P. Allis & Co. of Milwaulkee, U.S.A. The substations had static transformers and rotary converters, also by 1904, Margate Substation had batteries with 265 Tudor cells, twelve transformers and four converters, half of which were used for lighting purposes. Traction current was supplied at 500 volts and until the 1920s, the batteries provided power and lighting during the night, when the generators were shut down.

The car shed at St. Peters originally had room for 40 cars, being 231 feet long by 90 feet wide, with eight tracks, each having an inspection pit underneath. It was a large corrugated iron building, the roofing and ironwork being supplied by Messrs. Hill & Smith of London. As related elsewhere, there was subsequently a small depot at the Westbrook terminus as well.

The registered office of the Company was in London, originally at No. 7 Poultry but changed to 74 Cheapside on 28th April 1900. In later years the company had its head office at Moorgate Station Chambers, in the City of London, in the same building as the Provincial Tramways Group, but there is no reason to suppose a financial connection between them, except that in the 1920s, J. Barber Glenn was secretary of both organizations.

The Route Described

As completed, the Thanet main line started in Canterbury Road, Westbrook, which formerly in open country, is now a pleasant residential road and at the terminus, there was a trailing connection into a small depot, (opened 1902), set between houses. Soon, the line passed over a railway bridge and rounding a wide curve came out onto the sea front near Margate Stations; "Margate Sands" was on the sea front and "Margate West" set back slightly. The former was closed in 1926 and the other is now just "Margate". Close by is the

82. Above—A pre-war view of No. 8 in a rural setting in Lower North-down Road (now Northdown Park Road).

D. W. K. Jones.

83. Below—No. 24 in the 1930s on the roadside reservation of North-down Hill near the depot. Once a bleak open area, houses are now visible in the background and a builder's board stands uncomfortably in the foreground. D. W. K. Jones.

84. Opposite—A general view of St. Peters depot in the early 1930s.

N. D. W. Elston.

Dreamland Amusement Park, (formerly the "Hall by the Sea.") The tramline continued along the sea front, known as the Marine Terrace, passed on the seaward side of a large Clock Tower and turned north into the Marine Drive, towards the Harbour. After this the line turned slightly inland and divided into two one way tracks on a fairly steep gradient in narrow streets; running eastbound via Paradise Street and Fort Road (now widened) and westbound via Fort Hill and King Street. The one way section was followed by Fort Crescent with interlaced track and Ethelbert Terrace, both with hotels on the right and cliff top gardens on the left. A short distance along the latter, the trams made a right-angle turn inland into Athelstan Road, where the track became single. This led into Northdown Road, the main street of Cliftonville, the more fashionable part of the Borough of Margate.

The first part of Northdown Road is lined on both sides by shops and hotels but near the far end, after passing the church and a section where the tracks were too close together to permit cars to pass, building thinned out and the tramline made a further right turn to the south, this time on a narrow private reservation between hedges, to reach Lower Northdown Road (now Northdown Park Road). This soon became a narrow lane with tree branches touching the upper decks of the cars as they passed. At the "Wheatsheaf" public house the line entered another reservation, with trees on one side (now made up as St. Mary's Avenue) and then continued in a southerly direction down Northdown Hill, on which it crossed over and ran as a roadside reservation against the cornfields. The country here was very much more open then than now.

At the foot of Northdown Hill, in the outskirts of the village of St. Peters, the company's principal depot was located on the right, at the corner where the line turned left into Westover Road; it then turned sharp right into Beacon Road, where there was single track over a hump-back railway bridge, then into Albion Road, running under the shadow of the railway embankment and through St. Peters Park Road to Broadstairs, where the two tram lines divided.

The "Top Road" route crossed straight over Broadstairs Broadway into Osborne Rd. at the end of which there was a sharp right and left turn into Gladstone Road. Both of these roads are residential, but at the end of Gladstone Road, the line crossed over Ramsgate Road at Bromstone Corner onto the most extensive reservation on the system, on which the double track tram line ran through open country over the downs. After crossing the railway at the tunnel mouth, the "Top Road" line was rejoined by the "Main Line" at a junction still in open country. The section just described was always known officially as "Salisbury Avenue" although not made up as a road until long after the trams had disappeared.

In the meantime, the "Main Line" had turned left where it parted from the "Top Road" and passed under the bridge at Broadstairs Station, which had to be altered before the trams could run. The tram line continued down part of Broadstairs High Street, Queens Road and Oscar Road onto the sea front, known as Victoria Parade, thence along Westcliff Avenue behind the Grand Hotel, onto a section of private reservation across country to rejoin the "Top Road." This section and that next to be described, were named "Dumpton Park Drive" and are now made up.

The main reservation over the downs had rows of stone setts on either side of the rails and earth between them. The overhead wires were suspended from centre posts between the tracks. The line descended into the outskirts of Ramsgate, in later years passing the Greyhound Stadium and crossed Thanet Road into Bellevue Road, which was rather narrow and on a gradient. On the lower part, there was double track but the two sets of rails were too close together for cars to pass each other. At the bottom, the line turned left into a street lined with Georgian houses and shops, which rejoices in the peculiar name "The Plains of Waterloo" and then out onto the collonaded Wellington Crescent at cliff top level. From here it descended the steep and winding Madeira Walk with artificial rocks and water falls on the right and the backs of hotels on the left. At the bottom, the line skirted round the harbour, where there was a short siding onto the quayside and then followed the Royal Parade and Paragon up against the brick reinforced cliffs, with a three tier promenade effect, and thus into St. Augustine's Road overshadowed by a large convent and still climbing. Hereafter, the trams turned inland into Grange Road

Broadstairs.

85. Upper—Car No. 59 with two-pane vestibule passing under Broadstairs station bridge, which had to be altered before the trams could run under it, delaying the opening of the sea front route. Note board warning passengers to keep their seats under the bridge.   C. Carter.

86. Lower—Cars on the private track between Broadstairs and Ramsgate, looking back towards Broadstairs Infirmary. Note the centre posts carrying the overhead wires and the unmade roadway in open country.
D. W. K. Jones.

which gradually became narrower and more suburban. At the narrow-est point, iron railings and bushes on the right denoted Ellington Park.

The tram line bore round to the right beside the park into St. Lawrence High Street and Park Road, (also known as Ellington Park Road) to finish in the forecourt of the then Ramsgate Town Station, having completed three quarters of a circle round the town of Ramsgate.

The Thanet tram route running for much of its length alongside seaside gardens and on tree-lined or cross country reservations, must have been one of the most picturesque in the country and this may well account for the fact that it is better represented on postcards than any other British tramway.

Inspection and Opening

In anticipation of the opening of the system, Mr. Arthur A. Tylor was appointed General Manager and Mr. Richard Humphries A.M.I.E.E. was appointed Engineer.

Experimental runs were taking place in March 1901, after trials in a blizzard near Ramsgate. Driver training was mostly done on Car No. 22, one of the bogie cars and these cars found out the inaccuracies of gauge at the bends. At certain points along the route, such as the climb from Ramsgate Harbour up Madeira Walk, large crowds gathered to cheer derailments at the waterfall. Drivers and conductors received no pay until the end of their eight weeks training period; a fair proportion of them were local men, but the bulk of the manpower was Irish, some of whom had come over to work on the construction. The original cost of construction was £450,000 to which had to be added £9,261 as the cost of extensions.

The Board of Trade Inspection took place on Friday 29th March; official approval was received and the line was opened for traffic from Margate Stations to Ramsgate Harbour, via the "Top Road" on the Thursday before Easter, 4th April 1901. Only eight cars were able to run on the first day, apparently because the sub-stations were not completed the power was lacking, particularly at the ends of the line.

Some forty years later, one of the conductors, Mr. Impett describes the scene:—

"Almost the entire population of the Isle of Thanet wanted a ride. They crowded on the cars, standing on the top deck, down both front and rear staircases, all through the inside, on both platforms and even on the buffers. We conductors were compelled to fight them with iron point shifters to prevent more hanging on to the steps, for thousands were scrambling to get on. Imagine if you can the plight of the greenhorn conductors trying to take fares; No one knew what the change was; two tickets had to be issued for the return journey.

Our punches, turned by a wheel which took the skin off your thumb and fingers. Everyone of course, offered silver and you had no change except the 2s. 6d. which you had been given to start the day with.
Everyone was pushing you about. The trolley rope hung down through the back window, and every now and then, there not being sufficient tension on the trolley pole spring, or because someone was lying against the rope, the trolley would fly off the wire and you would have to leave your fares and put it back again. I am afraid many on that first trip did not pay at all and others travelled all the way from Margate to Ramsgate on a penny ticket. In addition to our own troubles we conductors had to lay 'fish plates' and help the driver to get the tram back on the track each time it left the rails. Although I was a very fit young fellow at the time and a very experienced footballer I think I did more shoulder charging during the Easter holidays of 1901 than during the whole of my career on the football field."

This is the background to the comment by 'Tramway and Railway World' that it was "one of the most interesting and unique installations that have yet been completed in this country" and mentioning the provision of light, power and traction from a single station and the interurban character of the line. It would "provide local travelling facilities for a district that hitherto possessed no means of communication except those provided by an infrequent and erratic train service," and would not have been possible but for the Light Railways Act and "the enterprising initiative of Mr. Murphy". It was pointed out that more than three miles of new roads had been constructed, nearly two miles doubled and remade, not to mention the construction of a new railway bridge over High Street Broadstairs without interrupting the train service (which task had not then been accomplished!)

In spite of all the free rides and shortage of power over 9,000 fares were accounted for daily over the Easter holiday. As yet, however, the line was only open from Margate Station (L.C. & D.R.) to Ramsgate Harbour.

On 5th May, the remarkable feat was accomplished of replacing the bridge at Broadstairs Station in the early hours of the Sunday morning without interrupting the train service.

There were at first no regular stopping places, and under the Order the cars were required to 'stop for the taking up and setting down of passengers as and when any passenger shall reasonably require.' This apparently included being asked to stop at the front door of a house to set down the mistress and a few yards further on to set down the maid at the back door! As difficult as the rich in their own way were the large families who used to arrive in Margate by boat and go on by tram to Ramsgate where accommodation was cheaper. These would scatter those of their children over five throughout the vehicle and forget to pay for them.

Madeira Walk.

87. Looking down Madeira Walk, showing Car No. 4 ascending, Ramsgate Harbour and the three-tier effect of the Royal Parade on the far side, with another car just visible on the horizon.

Frith photo Courtesy A. D. Packer.

The local Press adopted a somewhat hostile tone; "they will lessen the profits of some flymen and some brake proprietors, besides frightening our horses, adding a new terror to cyclists, and wrenching vehicles generally." Indeed the local flymen lost much business when the trams arrived to do the journey from Margate Station to Cliftonville for a penny, and did their best to obstruct the track. More than one cab was smashed in this 'war'.

The remaining portions of the electric tramway were opened on 6th July 1901.

As soon as the line was opened, it became evident that more cars could be used in the summer months and twenty more were ordered. In June 1901, it was reported that the British Thomson-Houston Company had the order in hand; the cars were to be mounted on Brill 21E trucks and to have standard B.T-H. equipment. Because of the slow delivery of American cars, the first ten were ordered from George F. Milnes & Co. of Hadley, Shropshire and to speed delivery, ten more bodies were added to an order in hand for Chatham; thus Nos. 41-50 which were delivered in July, were almost identical with Chatham Nos. 1-25. These were allocated to the "Top Road" service from Broadstairs to Ramsgate Harbour, being nicknamed the "Loopers" and their bodies were narrower than the rest of the fleet. The other ten cars came later from the British Electric Car Co., in which Mr. Murphy was a major shareholder. These latter cars had partially vestibuled platforms with windscreens at the ends only and open at the sides, which made them rather draughty and consequently they were nicknamed the "Airships".

These extra cars required further accommodation and although two short roads were added at St. Peters Depot, close to the railway, this was insufficient and a plot of land was obtained by the Westbrook terminus, on a 99 year lease from the Bridewell Hospital at an annual rental of £12 10s. 0d. This small brick and corrugated iron shed had the track connection towards Westgate, which suggested that the Company still had hopes of extending the line in that direction. Its location did enable the company to start some early morning journeys from Westbrook, giving a more balanced build-up to the service (illustration on page 220).

When the tramway was open from end to end, two basic services were worked:—

(a) Westbrook-Margate-Cliftonville-St. Peters-Broadstairs (Sea Front)-Ramsgate Harbour-St. Lawrence-Ramsgate Town Station.

(b) Broadstairs Broadway-Gladstone Road-Dumpton Park-Ramsgate Harbour.

Service (a) was known as the "Main Line" and service (b) as the "Top Road".

Cars on the latter started in Osborne Road and terminated on the short spur line at Ramsgate Harbour. There were also various short workings on the main line to meet particular traffic requirements.

It has been suggested that it had been the original intention of the company to operate an "express" service from Margate to Ramsgate via the "Top Road" using the bogie cars and to operate local services, including the sea front at Broadstairs with the four wheelers. However, the unreliable performance of the bogie cars caused the company to have second thoughts and apart from the first few weeks, while awaiting the completion of Broadstairs Station bridge, through cars did not run via the "Top Road" except when going into service from the depot to Ramsgate.

The Accident-Prone Tramway: 1901-1905

In September 1905 a London paper was quoted locally as saying that "there had been no deaths in Ramsgate that week, which was surprising considering the existence of the tramway." Certainly the

88. Car No. 29 descending the gradient in King Street, Margate. Note the interlaced track going into one way in different streets, the signal worked by an official standing at the base of the post and the stop sign "Downhill cars stop here".   Late Dr. Hugh Nicol.

first four and a half years had more than their fair share of accidents. On 24th April 1901 the first injury occurred when the trolley came off as a car was ascending Madeira Walk. The car, running back, stayed on the track, but a Mr. Abrams jumped off and suffered a fractured arm. Five days later after a shower of rain a car ran away down the hill and crashed into the kerb about fifty yards from the bottom, damaging the axle and one wheel. While the breakdown gang were at work there was a second addition to the excitement of the crowd; "a second car ascending the hill suddenly rushed backwards. Providentially it safely negotiated the corner, and was stopped at the terminus at the bottom of York Street." The following day one of the drivers knocked himself out on one of the posts just past East Cliff Lodge on the way to Broadstairs; three days later a car going towards the Westbrook terminus, ran into the fence just after passing over the railway bridge and nearly went down the bank.

Ramsgate Corporation met early in May 1901 to discuss the situation, mentioning the frequent accidents, the inexperience of the drivers and "the abominable way in which Mr. Murphy had left the sides of the wood paving, both in St. Augustine's Road and Grange Road" also commenting that "it was not very courteous to keep the trams at the bottom of Harbour Street, blocking up the road just as they liked." They agreed to write to the Board of Trade for an inquiry. Margate Council met soon afterwards, but confined mention of the company to the fact that various street works had been helped by the £3,500 deposited by it.

Meanwhile on Whit Monday 26,000 passengers were carried and on the following Wednesday, 29th May 1901, the extension to Ellington Park, Ramsgate was opened. Bye-laws and Regulations published on 1st June declared that in future, entry and departure was to be from the rear platform only; smoking was prohibited inside; numbers carried were to be limited and a notice was to be displayed when cars were full.

On 15th June the Board of Trade Inquiry took place. Many people wished to complain, among them being the vicar of St. Paul's Church, Margate, who said he was unable to conduct the service for the noise (there was never any suggestion that cars should not run on Sundays); but the Inquiry was confined to accidents. At one corner, by No. 11 Ethelbert Crescent, Cliftonville, — nine cars had been de-railed during the previous week. Although it was one of the small cars which had been derailed at both ends of the adjoining Athelstan Road while full of yeomanry, it was the "bogey" cars (sic) which were generally blamed. It was suggested that they had been obtained to make up for the restriction on trailers. Broken axles, trolley arms leaving the wires and the closeness of the tracks near the Imperial Hotel, Cliftonville, were mentioned as well, but the company claimed that the trouble had almost stopped and that 700,000 passengers had been carried and 140,000 miles covered in ten weeks.

The inexperience of drivers came in for some comment; they were paid 4/- a day with a 6d. bonus for experienced men. Conductors received 3/1d. a day. Not all the staff excelled in electrical knowledge — according to one story told later, the breakdown gang were sent out to look for the car which took the staff to Ramsgate at midnight, only to find the driver sitting waiting in Thanet Road for the current to come on. The trolley wheel was resting on the strain wire!

Broadstairs Council discussed the smoke nuisance from the power station at St. Peters and Ramsgate Corporation decided to proceed against the Company for illegal display of advertisements and in August Major Pringle's report appeared — The quality of steel used in the American cars was criticised; axles had had to be replaced by English steel ones and a trolley mast had broken, owing to a flaw in the casting. Much trouble had been caused by adverse camber at both ends of Athelstan Road, Margate and at the junction of Fort Road and King Street, also by the very sharp radius of some curves. It was suggested that the reverse curve in Fort Road should be straightened and various inaccuracies attended to. The reversed bogies of the larger cars came in for severe comment. It was suggested that the points of support for the load were only 11 feet apart and the platforms overhung by 10 feet 8 inches and therefore the trucks should be turned round and thus increase the effective wheelbase to 13 feet 4 inches and reduce the overhang to 9 feet 6 inches.

Then on 10th August, just before 7.30 p.m., came the first serious accident. Car No. 8 ran away down Fort Hill, Margate, nearly full with sparks flying from locked wheels and overturned into the shop fronts of Nos. 8 & 10 King Street, injuring 28 people. The staff car No. 38 came with jacks and chains and put No. 8 back on the track, after which it was driven back to the depot. But, at 9.20 p.m. No. 50 was sent with tools and implements to clear up the mess; its brakes also failed and it ran into No. 38, fortunately without further injury. Another Inquiry took place and revealed that the hill was protected by a semaphore signal at the top, worked by an inspector and a man was kept at the top to sand the rails. The driver of No. 50 qualified as a driver in Dublin and attributed skidding down hill to wet rails and pedestrian traffic. The driver of No. 8 had had 16 days instruction and said he might have put the controller handle in the wrong direction.

The Report of the Inquiry, published in November, required the Company to put slipper brakes on all cars, to provide a speed indicator with a governor to shut off current at 12 miles per hour and to limit the speed anywhere on the system to 10 m.p.h. The limit was the usual one at the time; in fact most were limited to eight m.p.h., although by 1904, the Board of Trade were prepared to raise this to 12 m.p.h. for most systems. Thanet were still limited to 10, while Chatham and Dover were kept at 8 m.p.h. In June 1902, the Company was fined £5 for allowing their cars to be driven at over 16 m.p.h. and required to take 75 minutes instead of one hour to run from terminus to terminus (68 to 75 minutes were still allowed in 1936).

Mr. Tylor left the Company in February 1902 and by the beginning of 1904, Mr. Humphries had been confirmed in both posts of Manager & Engineer.

The company hastened to fit track brakes and all the four wheel cars were so fitted by about September 1902. The brakes were of the B.E.C. patent type, operated by a hand-wheel surrounding the hand-brake staff on the platform; they performed well on tests carried out on Fort Road, Margate. The eight-wheel cars with their reversed bogies presented more of a problem, however. A track brake between the wheels would cause the front wheels to lift up off the track, as only about 30% of the weight of the car was on them. The solution was a novel and unique one, designed by Mr. Humphries. A pair of steel scotches were fitted in front of each pair of the large wheels at each end of the car. They were worked independent of each other from the platform. When released, the scotch was pressed by a spring between the wheel and the track, the spring tended to force the scotch under the wheel and bring onto it the weight carried by the wheel. So long as the wheels were revolving, this was effective in preventing the cars from running away. In the event of a run-back, they were to be applied by the conductor and if the car ran forwards, they were to be applied by the driver.

As by then troubles with the track were mostly solved, and the promised Workmen's cars had started in June, it might have been thought that the Company's problems were at an end. However, a petition by ratepayers complained of the noise made by the bogie cars; it was promised that they would be taken off by November 1902. Nevertheless, they were still running in the following year and Ramsgate Council were deciding to approach the Board of Trade, when on the evening of Wednesday 12th August 1903, two of the cars collided in Bellevue Road, Ramsgate and thirty people were injured. The gradient here was 1 in 30 with a ninety yard stretch of 1 in 12 and although the track was double, there was a ninety yard section over which the rails were too close together for cars to pass each other. Descending cars were required to wait at a marked pole for cars coming up, but on this occasion, the descending car with its trolley dewired, failed to stop in time. The driver of the ascending car reversed but only managed to lessen the shock. There followed yet another inquiry, at which most of the criticism was levelled at the

Thanet Accidents.

89. Above—Car No. 47 when it ran into a shop at the Plains of Waterloo. Evidently more damage was done to the building than the car.

Courtesy J. H. Price.

90. Below—The remains of No. 41 on the beach at Ramsgate after it fell over the cliff from Madeira Walk. The separated truck and broken platform bearers are clearly visible.

Photo by A. Wallis. Courtsy N. D. W. Elston.

special track brake on the bogie cars. It could not be screwed down as could a slipper brake, before commencing to run down a steep hill and evidently in fact Driver Collins had never thought of using it while running down hill. Lieut. Col. P. G. von Donop, R.E. concluded his report by saying, "The problem must be faced, or the use of these cars discontinued". He added that all cars must be able to stop and apply their slipper brakes at a compulsory stop in Albion Street on the downward journey.

Thus the Company was faced with a dilemma; the bogie cars were unsuitable for the fitting of track brakes on the type of bogie used, yet on the other hand, the bodies of the cars were too long to ride on any four wheel truck then known. The only solution found possible, and a drastic one, was to shorten the bodies of the cars and mount them on standard single trucks. Thus twenty Brush four wheel trucks were ordered in April 1904, to be fitted with ordinary screw down slipper brakes. Then one at a time, the twenty bogie cars were taken apart and re-assembled only four and a half windows long. In fact they finished a foot shorter than Nos. 1-20. The operation took many months to complete, cost £1,833, the greater part of which was written off in six annual instalments. In May 1904, the Company advertised in "Tramway & Railway World" twenty pairs of Saint Louis maximum traction trucks in good order — a bargain! However, this type of bogie was never used on any other British tramway, but was used on a few German systems. A car still on bogies was noted in September 1904.

If the trams were having their own troubles, they were also blamed for those of the local railway and the Manager of the S.E. & C.R. took the opportunity of the Light Railway Inquiry, held at Dartford in February 1903 to say that he regarded tramways as a great peril, which had caused a considerable fall in traffic on the railway between Margate, Broadstairs and Ramsgate. Two years later 'Keble's Gazette' was remarking that "Our tramway has ruined our local railway. The nemesis is coming fast, and motor cars will ruin the tramways." In September 1905 he was forecasting that motor buses would take over, and remarking on the change from private houses to shops along the tram route.

Meanwhile, in 1903 Mr. Humphries was marketing his own design of sleeve for splicing trolley wires, consisting of two halves and a small union to join the halves together. Soldering could be done at any time. "Every tramway engineer knows the difficulty (to put it mildly) of joining the ends of a broken trolley wire in the pouring rain or with the thermometer below freezing point." Familiar words to those who have experienced the cold winds that blow over the island in the winter. Indeed the weather had a perennial effect on the system. Annual reports frequently blamed a drop in receipts on 'inclement weather' in the early years, and when in February 1905 the Board of Trade published new regulations which apart from discouraging centre poles and reversed staircases forbade the use of top deck covers on lines of 3′ 6″ gauge or less, Mr. Humphries commented that he thought the prohibition unfair. "If a roof cover is allowed subject to the overhang of the car it would be a very different thing. With reasonable overhang I am sure that roof covers would not be a danger, as the centre of gravity of a heavy car is so low." As it was, the centre of gravity was anything but low as passengers crowded onto the top deck to enjoy the sun — so many of them that extra drivers had to be taken on.

This brought further problems in 1905. On 27th May No. 47 ran away down the hill to the Plains of Waterloo in Ramsgate and failed to take the bend. It fetched up in a grocer's shop, seriously injuring the manager's seven year old daughter as well as the driver and conductor, and had to be left there until the shop was shored up. Ramsgate Council commented that "Accidents were causing Ramsgate a great deal of harm, for people might think Ramsgate was quite a dangerous place to come to."

Then on 3rd August No. 41 came down Madeira Walk out of control in the rain, broke through an iron fence and fell some 32 feet over the cliff into temporarily unoccupied ground at the rear of the Queen's Head public house. Fortunately there were only six passengers on the car, and the only person seriously injured was the driver, who jumped off before it went over but fell on his head. The inquiry, conducted by Col. von Donop, revealed that the driver had been employed as a motorman for only nine days previous to the accident and had been allowed to take cars up and down Madeira Walk from the first day. The sanding gear had failed to operate and its design was criticised because sand did not fall on the rails when the car was going round a curve. The wheels had locked with the handbrake, rendering the rheostatic brake inoperative, and the slipper brake, usually applied by means of a wheel which gave the driver a chance to compensate for worn blocks, was in this case applied by means of a lever with a screw adjustment which was of no use in an emergency and made no allowance for brake wear during a journey. The super-elevation at the point where the car came off was ½″ in the wrong direction, and the wheel flanges were chipped to only ¼″ deep in places. The company had tried steel tyres but on the Ramsgate curves the flanges had only lasted a month. The car had been thoroughly overhauled and re-wheeled in December 1904.

By this time nearly 340,000 journeys on Madeira Walk had been made, and the tramway had carried more than 4¼ million passengers a year, but it was decided that the track should be improved at this point and that in future only experienced drivers should be employed on the hills. In this accident, car No. 41 was damaged beyond repair

214

and broken up. Later, car No. 47 was patched up with parts of No. 41 and sent out again, but on the first journey it ran away down High Street Broadstairs and hit a coal lorry which fortunately prevented it from going through a shop window at the corner of Queen's Road. After this accident there was some reluctance on the part of drivers to take it out again; but there are no more such incidents to report.

1906 was almost entirely free from accidents, which was attributed in the annual report to the fact that only the most experienced motor-men were allowed to drive the cars on steep gradients. A start was made on improvements to the line on Madeira Walk, which eventually cost £2,019/11/4d. Tramway affairs settled down now; profits which had been £60,299 in the first full year of operation in 1902 varied from £31,336 in 1908 (blamed on "inclement weather in August and September") to £37,365 in 1911 when "the weather during the past summer was exceptionally fine."

The main development during these years was in the electric lighting business and to cope with extra demand, a gas engine was installed in 1906, a new sub-station built at Cliftonville in 1908 and another at Broadstairs in 1912. The Manager, Mr. Humphries, left in January 1907, to become manager of the Malta Tramways and was replaced at Thanet by Mr. J. A. Forde, A.M.I.E.E., who stayed until the closure thirty years later.

1907 saw the removal of the centre posts from Marine Drive and Marine Terrace, Margate. They had been unpopular from the start and even before the line opened, the division of the road was claimed to make the whole sea front unsafe for driving. The increase in motor traffic made them more of a menace and after a series of letters in the local paper, Margate Town Council decided on 9th July to pay half the cost of their removal, up to a maximum of £90.

In 1911 a new scale of fares came into operation in April and the press commented favourably on the new 1d. fare from Broadstairs front to St. Peters. The same year saw the Coronation of King George V on 2nd June, when one of the B.E.C. cars was specially decorated. Also, a profit of £21,785 was made on the year's opera-tion. Unfortunately in April 1912, there was a coal strike, after which Mr. Forde was presented with a set of golf clubs and a bag, by the employees, grateful because by "great foresight" he had kept not only the cars running but all the men at work. Industrial relations were notably good under Mr. Forde's management, but the fact that the condition of the cars had deteriorated, was shown on 17th August, when the French aviator M. Samlet demonstrated his aeroplane in a field opposite the power station. All fifty-nine cars were brought out, but as described long afterwards, "some had one flat wheel, some two, some had two flats on one wheel and some were almost without wheels at all. They came along making a terrific clatter all the way with their life guards touching the ground because of the weight of the crowds riding on them. — It was a great day." But there do not seem to have been any modifications to the trams in this period beyond placing the destination boards on the upper deck screens instead of on the dash. A. J. Bousfield became Assistant Manager in 1911.

In 1913 the Company bought three motor-buses and at last achieved its aim of taking traffic from Birchington, frustrated hitherto by the exclusiveness of the Westgate private estate, which kept out the trams and forbade excursion trains. The buses only brought in £348 in 1913 and were probably second-hand vehicles. There was already competition from other operators as the Isle of Thanet Motor Co. Ltd. of 1 York Terrace, Ramsgate, were running a service with four motor coaches and two char-a-bancs between Margate and Ramsgate.

Lean Years — The Great War

Annual Reports for these years speak for themselves:—

"On 31st July 1914, traffic takings showed an increase from 31st October 1913, to date, of £1,255-3-10d. compared with the same ten months in the previous financial year, but upon the declaration of war on 4th August, an exodus of the visitors immediately commenced and traffic receipts fell largely from day to day."

"The prospects of the Company were most promising when they were suddenly affected by the outbreak of war."

"The Company had just completed large extensions to their generating plant and were in an excellent position to meet the growing demand for light and power, also the growing traffic on the tramways. . ."

Later in the war, a Report read dismally:—

"The Company's operations during the last year (1917) have been carried on under the most trying circumstances — attacks from enemy raiders on Ramsgate, Margate and Broadstairs — loss of life, personal injuries and material damage — with the result that not only have visitors, who are the Company's main source of income, ceased to frequent these pleasant resorts, but many residents who were electric light consumers have closed their homes and gone to reside elsewhere." A loss of £4,731 was made in 1917.

The undertaking was kept going by loans from the Directors and the Secretary, while Debenture stockholders were called together and sanctioned the issue of £35,000 Prior Loan Stock. In 1914 receipts were £33,714 on the trams and, a record £11,648 from electricity, with the buses taking £397. In 1918, these figures were almost halved to £16,614, £5,055 and £388 respectively. On 29th May 1918, the offices and stores were destroyed by a fire, but the cars and power station were saved. Improvement came shortly after the end of the war, although coal was still in short supply, but things were looking better, when on 17th July 1919, Mr. Murphy died. He had been a member of the Board since 1902 and it was said that the Company always had the benefit of his grasp of affairs, his business capacity and his special knowledge. Mr. J. Barber Glenn took his place as Chairman.

Postwar — Renovation

The end of the war saw the cars and track in a very bad condition. Cars which had already been in bad condition before the war, were canibalized extensively to keep the others going, but now only 14 were in running order. The track too was in bad condition; a rail-grinding machine was hired from the Woods Gilbert Rail Remodelling Company of Bolton in 1919, to get rid of the worst of the corrugations. It was impossible to overhaul all the cars at once and there ensued a policy of gradual improvement which lasted until the closure of the system. Cars were taken in for repair and rebuilt extensively, an additional coachbuilder being taken on for the purpose. Some cars acquired Peckham "Pendulum" trucks and other trucks were changed round. Some bodies, which can be seen from photographs of the time, with drooping platforms and (because entrances were on opposite sides at each end), a distinct twist in the body — were placed on jacks taking a night or two to regain their former shape. However, this "do it yourself" policy meant that a car could be rebuilt at a cost of £375 as against £650 for a new car body. About 1925, the experiment was tried of replacing mahogany side panels with aluminium ones supplied by the British Aluminium Company. Car No. 36 was the first to be so treated, but it was not a complete success, as when the ends of the car drooped again, the panel was inclined to split.

During the early 1920s, two of the Milnes cars, Nos. 42 and 45 had their staircases removed and the entrances altered to the nearside-front to permit one-man operation. In this condition they were used for a time on the "Top Road". No. 45 was later cut down to a single decker. (See Rolling Stock section for further details).

Decline 1920s & 1930s

In 1924, powers were obtained to supply electricity to Westgate & Birchington; it was plain that the electric supply side of the business was the chief concern of the company, when in June, the name was changed to the "Isle of Thanet Electric Supply Company". Even so it was only in the 1920s that the generator kept running all night — until then any nocturnal load as well as the early morning trams, had been supplied from batteries. For all this the trams were well turned out in their later years.

During this period trams ran every few minutes on the main line in summer, but by comparison, an hourly service was sufficient, worked by one car, on the "Top Road", where traffic was very light indeed.

In the meantime, the Southern Railway Company which had taken over from the former South Eastern & Chatham Railways, was rationalizing its lines in the Thanet area. On 2nd July 1926, Ramsgate Harbour station and the tunnel leading down into it were closed and

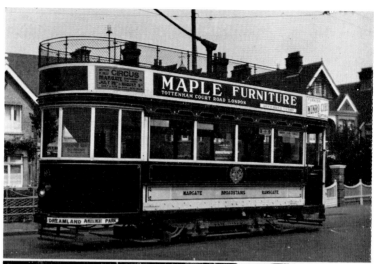

Rebuilding in the 1920s.

91. Upper—No. 10 in the final livery, resplendent on a new Peckham "Pendulum" truck.   R. Elliott.

92. Lower—No. 31 awaiting rebuilding and a new vestibule being built onto another car as yet anonymous.   D. W. K. Jones.

218

the line from Margate via Broadstairs, which had terminated there was diverted via Dumpton Park to a new "through" Ramsgate Town Station, set about half a mile back from its predecessor. At the same time the direct line from Margate Sands to Ramsgate Town was closed, but for some long time after this, the trams continued to terminate rather uselessly on what had become a short section of reserved track in the empty forecourt of the disused Ramsgate Town Station. At some later date, certainly after 1930, it is believed that the cars did not run to the end of the track, but terminated further back in Park Road, slightly nearer to the new station.

Bus Operation

The notable feature of the post-war years was the expansion of the motor bus system, until eventually the Company had more buses running than trams. The effect of intensive bus competition had been felt as early as 1921 and there followed a period of intensive rivalry with the East Kent Company in which several smaller fleets were bought out on either side.* By 1931, the tram company owned 35 buses mostly Thornycrofts, but including one ex-London "B" type double-decker. The services operated included a lengthy circular route, which took in Birchington and Pegwell Bay, on which there was a bargain fare of 1/6d. for a ride right round the circle from any point back to the same point, 20 miles in all. (See list of services and fleet list in Appendix I.) A garage was built in 1928.

Six of the Thornycroft buses were open toppers and the rest were single deckers of 20 and 32 seat capacities. In 1929 five Daimler single deck and two open top buses were purchased. Subsequently a batch of 24 Daimler 32 seat single deck buses was acquired from the associated Lanarkshire Traction Co. in Scotland, then being taken over by the S.M.T. Finally in 1936, the Company bought seven fine modern looking Daimler covered top double deck buses to replace the Thornycroft open toppers. Bus services were operated mainly at half-hourly intervals and used both as feeders to the tramways and to counter competition. The staff remained at work during the General Strike in 1926

Some Improvements

The capital was increased by £140,000 to £500,000 in February 1926.

In 1927 a brighter livery was adopted, red for the trams and emerald green for the buses. (See note at end of chapter for details). The Lanarkshire buses were already in a similar green livery. A further improvement was made when a stock of coat of arms transfers was discovered and once again appeared on the sides of the trams and

---

*Including the West Margate Coach Co., taken over in 1921, with 2 A.E.C. single deckers and two double deck ex-London "B" type. Carlton Coaches acquired in 1925 had three Berliet single deckers.

buses. In 1931 Westbrook depot ceased to be used as a running shed and was used to store unserviceable cars.

Labour relations in the company were excellent; the custom was that all those members of the staff who maintained the trams during the winter months were required to drive or conduct them in the summer season. In fact, during the summer it was rare to see both the driver and the conductor in uniform. On occasion Mr. Forde himself would be found acting as driver or even as a meter reader. Other senior men were required to relieve inexperienced drivers on hills or to act as inspectors at places like Margate Station, when trams might arrive in bunches and had to be turned short of the terminus. The spring points were normally held by rubber inserts which had to be removed and a lever used when required.

The Closure

The reasons for the final closure were complex, but chiefly related to the hostility of the local authorities and to the fact that the electricity supply business was the dominant side of the Company's affairs. In 1930 a rumour of impending sale caused the price of shares to rise, but in 1933 an increase in electricity prices, made in January, caused considerable indignation among the public and Margate Council expressed the opinion that the electricity undertaking was subsidising the trams. In August that year they formed a Transport Committee and from then on the situation was constantly under review. In April 1935 Broadstairs, Ramsgate and Margate Councils agreed jointly to appoint an expert to advise on the situation (at a fee of not more than 150 guineas) and to share in any contribution the company might make towards the reinstatement of the roads. So, on 15th June 1935 "Transport World" (successor of "Tramway & Railway World") reported that the three local councils had decided to press the company to abandon the tramways in favour of motor buses.

At a General Meeting, held on 10th March 1935, the Chairman (Mr. Arthur Hoare, who had taken over over after the death of Mr. A. R. Monks in the previous April), reported that "the Company was recently requested by the Local Councils of Margate, Broadstairs and Ramsgate to consider also the abandonment of our tramway system and the substitution of motor omnibuses therefor. The matter which is closely allied to the question of the Company's electricity supply tenure, is now receiving the consideration of the Board."

The time was falling near when the electricity supply business could be bought out by the local authorities and the Company had, there-

93. Left—No. 25 on the humped back bridge over the railway in Beacon Road, St. Peters.   D. W. K. Jones.
94. Centre—A recent view of Westbrook Depot taken in 1967.
                                                                      J. H. Price.
95. Right—No. 24 in use as a snow plough during wintery weather in the 1920s.   Courtesy J. H. Price.

fore, no option. Financial affairs were healthy but the emphasis was on electricity supply; for example, in 1935 £3,818 was spent on track renewals, £1,519 on buses and £21,346 on electricity supply, chiefly for a new sub-station at Margate. Profits were £58,925 in 1933, £54,097 in 1934 and £50,098 in 1935, rising to £58,925 in 1936, the last full year of operation. Concurrently, ordinary shares paid a 4% dividend from 1927 onwards. It was said that the increase in the local electricity charges rising from £7,331 in 1933 to £19,303 in 1934 was equivalent to a 3% dividend on the ordinary shares.

In May 1936, the Company agreed to abandon the tramways not later than 31st March 1937, or as soon as an Order could be obtained and to replace them by motor-buses. In August, however, a stockholder's meeting agreed to sell their omnibus undertaking to the East Kent Road Car Co. Ltd., for £175,000 and from 1st October 1936, the Thanet buses were operated as agents for the East Kent company. Also in October it was announced that the local councils would receive £16,100, towards the reinstatement of the roads when the tram tracks had been lifted and in November, it was predicted that the abandonment would take place on 24th March 1937, just short of 36 years since the opening of the electric tramways.

Thus, the necessary preparations were put in hand and although the Company were unable to adhere exactly to the predicted date, the cars made their final runs on the night of Wednesday 27th March 1937. Last cars in each direction were driven by the Mayors of the towns through which they passed, with the Town Clerks acting as conductors — the actual final trip was made by car No. 20, amid the usual revelry, including a band and girls in conductors' uniforms. Mr. Forde was presented with a model tram.

The next morning, the services were operated by scarlet & cream East Kent Leyland "Titan" buses* bearing the route numbers 49 and 49A (the two services working opposite ways round a loop in Ramsgate). At a later date, a new service numbered 50 was introduced and partly covered the tram route.

The Thanet Company reported a loss of £87,000 on the transaction, having valued the undertaking at £245,869 and sold the buses for £175,000, while it had to pay £16,100 to the various local authorities towards the cost of removing the rails and repairing the carriageway. Considerable hardship was felt by employees who were retired without pension rights. A contractor from Dover obtained the rails in exchange for removing them and it is said, sold them to a German firm, so they probably came back in a different form during the war! In spite of an anonymous offer of £5 towards the preservation of one

---

*Until uniform liveries were imposed on nationalized bus undertakings in 1973, East Kent buses were painted deep scarlet and buff. Maidstone & District buses were dark sage green and ivory.

96. No. 58 with 3 pane partial vestibule in Ramsgate Town Station Yard.
G. L. Gundry.

---

of the cars, they were all "pulled apart at the depot" (presumably this means the bodies removed from the trucks) by two other cars, until the final ones were pulled apart by lorries. The depot building at St. Peters was handed over to the East Kent bus company for use as a garage and the 49 tram company's buses handed over were quickly repainted in East Kent livery.

Conditions in the area were even worse during the 1939-1945 war than during the 1914-1918 war; Mr. J. A. Forde J.P. and his wife were killed in an air-raid which demolished their house in 1941. After relinquishing management of the trams, he had remained with the Electricity undertaking and his place was now taken by Mr. T. A. Chell, who had been with the Company since 1912. It had been the intention of the local authorities to take over the electricity side of the business but because of the war, this was delayed until 1st January 1947, when the Margate, Broadstairs and District Electricity Board took over. However, its life was destined to be only one year as it was nationalized in 1948. The power station was demolished in 1967.

Like St. Peters Depot, Westbrook depot still stands and some track-work, including Askham's points are still in position. A few yards of track are still buried under the road surface on Fort Hill, Margate and there may be traces elsewhere. Ramsgate Council used the former traction poles in their area for gas street lighting and a few others still exist carrying cables, but not necessarily in their original positions, while a number of seats, stop signs and panels with coats of arms have

223

97. No. 12, one of the original St. Louis single truck cars in its condition as delivered.
Official photo

found their way into private collections. The Company was dissolved on 20th October 1952.

The short reserved track section at the end of Northdown Road is now a public footpath and although the Company paid £10,000 to Broadstairs Council to make up Salisbury Avenue and Dumpton Park Drive, thus absolving them of the statutory obligation to do this, the war intervened before the work was started and it was not completed until the 1960s. Thus the bus routes replacing the trams could not follow exactly the same routeing and in fact never have done so, except that an hourly service has been provided along Dumpton Park Drive since 1966. Otherwise they run on roads as nearly as possible parallel to the former tram route. The "Top Road" was not served.

ROLLING STOCK

Nos. 1-20. Built in 1900 and supplied in 1901.

Bodies built by ST. LOUIS CAR CO., St. Louis, U.S.A.

Dimensions — Saloon 17' 10" long 6' 6" wide. Overall length 29' 4".

Seating — 26 inside 29 outside. Total 55. 180° reversed stairs.

Electrical Equipment supplied by BRITISH THOMSON-HOUSTON CO. LTD.

Two B.T-H. G.E.58 motors of 35 horse power each.

Two B.T-H. B.18 type controllers.

Truck — ST. LOUIS cast frame type. 6' 0" wheelbase. (See also opposite.)

Braking — Hand, rheostatic and sprag. (See also opposite).

The saloons of these cars had four windows with rounded top corners each side and slit ventilators above leading to an internal clerestory. They were among the first to be delivered to a British tramway with enclosed vestibule fronts, which were glazed with five windows. Reversed stairs gave access to the upper deck which had the usual two and one reversible seats. Like all other Thanet cars, Nos. 1-20 retained their reversed stairs throughout their lives. The trolley mast which was offset towards one side and towards one end, was of an early Blackwell type, with an enclosed spring but no cap and known as the "Dublin" type; they were found to let in water and after a few years, a metal shield like an inverted shovel was fixed to the lower end of the trolley pole and covered the top of the mast. All Thanet cars had this type of mast. There was a single hand rail round the upper deck and the space between it and the decency panel was enclosed by wire netting. A lamp on a rather short stanchion stood at the stair head. Original drawings show a large oil headlamp on the dash, but as running the cars had electric headlamps on the upper deck canopy bend.

There was beading round the dash dividing it into two panels, corresponding with the waist and rocker panels of the saloon. Red cushioned seats ran the length of the saloon, which was entered by twin sliding doors and because of reflection from the glazed wind-screens, the bulkhead windows were painted over black and the glass in the door windows replaced by ply wood, in which a round hole was cut, so high up that although the driver could turn and peer at the passengers, they could not see out. Hickory comode handles were attached to the corner pillars next the platform step, but because the brake staff was set well back to clear the windscreen, there was not room for the usual central hand rail on the platform edge.

After the war, these cars required considerable rebuilding and in the process, lost the beading dividing the dash, the head lamp already having been transferred to the centre thereof. The St. Louis trucks had not proved entirely satisfactory and in any case spare parts for them were no longer available; consequently it was decided that as cars were overhauled they would be replaced by Brill 21.E trucks.

Nos. 3, 4, 9, 13 17 and 18 were evidently among the first cars to be rebuilt, appearing in the new red livery without coats of arms. Of these Nos. 4, 9 & 13 remained on St. Louis trucks, but photographs exist of No. 3 in the new livery on four different trucks (Brill — St. Louis — Brush and Peckham). Nos. 1 & 7 appeared on Brush "Aa" trucks evidently exchanged with cars of the 21-40 group while Nos. 5, 12, 14, 16, 17 and 19 finished up on 6' Brill 21E trucks. Finally, in the 1930s, Nos, 3, 6, 10 and 20 were mounted on more modern 6' 6" Peckham "Pendulum" trucks. All cars then had B.E.C. track brakes

98. A view of one of the bogie cars in its original condition.

Official photo.

similar to the "Spencer" type described on Page 154 Chap. 4, Vol. 1. Rebulit cars could be distinguished by the square top corners of the saloon and vestibule windows. Possibly Nos. 2, 8, 11 and 15 may have been canibalized to keep the others going. (A photograph of No. 18 in the new livery does not show the truck clearly).

Nos. 21-40.   Built in 1900 and supplied in 1901.

Bodies built by ST. LOUIS CAR CO. of St. Louis, U.S.A.

Dimensions — Saloon 21' 0" long, 6' 6" wide. Overall length 33' 4"

Seating 30 inside, 38 outside (as built). 180° reversed stairs.

Electrical equipment supplied by BRITISH THOMSON-HOUSTON CO. LTD.

Two B.T-H. G.E.58 motors of 35 horse power each.

Two B.T-H. B.18 controllers.

Bogies — ST. LOUIS reversed. type 13. 4' 0" wheelbase. Total wheelbase 16' 6".

Braking — Hand and rheostatic. (see opposite).

The bodies of these cars were generally similar to those of Nos. 1-20, but longer with six windows each side. The St. Louis bogies had the pony wheels towards the ends of the car. After a while they were fitted with "Scotch" brakes with which a triangular steel scotch could be pressed between the wheel and the rail by means of a spring, which was released by a small lever on the dash, by the driver when ascending a hill and by the conductor when descending. However on 12th August 1903, a bogie car equipped with this brake was involved in a serious accident, after which it was decided that in view of several steep gradients on this system, all cars must be equipped with proper track brakes which could be screwed down. It was found impracticable to fit them to this type of bogie without the risk of the pony wheels lifting and causing a derailment and on the other hand, the bodies were too long to fit on any type of four wheeled truck then known. Consequently the drastic step was taken of cutting them down. Each body was dismantled, part of one end cut from the saloon and the bulkhead reinstated, leaving a saloon only $4\frac{1}{2}$ windows long. As each window was slightly shorter than those on Nos. 1-20, these cars finished up one foot shorter than the first series. The shortened bodies were mounted on new Brush "Aa" trucks, fitted with B.E.C. track brakes like Nos. 1-20.

At one time No. 24 was fitted up for use as a snow plough.

They were subjected to the same rebuilding as the earlier batch, after the war and at that stage, some of the trucks seem to have been changed round, so that latterly Nos. 21, 22, 23, 27, 28, 30, 34 & 37 were on Brush "Aa" trucks while Nos. 24, 25, 29, 31, 35 and 39 were on Brill 21E trucks, all of 6 ft. wheelbase. Nos. 28 and 37 appeared in the new livery without coats of arms, so were apparently among the first to be rebuilt. However, when it came to the turn of No. 40, it was rebuilt more extensively than the others and emerged in 1927, repillared with four windows each side like Nos. 1-20. At this time it was one of the cars to receive aluminium side panelling and was mounted on a truck of the Peckham "Pendulum" type of 6 ft. 6 in. wheelbase.

Photographs of Nos. 26, 32 and 36 in the new livery do not show the trucks clearly, but no photo exists of No. 38 in the new livery and it may have been broken up for spare parts.

Note—Nos. 1-20 & 21-40, were "knocked down" and shipped over in crated parts from America to be assembled on arrival in Great Britain. The Brush "Aa" and the Brill 21E trucks, with which cars of these classes were later fitted were closely similar in design and axle boxes and other parts appear to have been exchanged between them in later years.

Correction to map on page 186, for Salisbury Road, Broadstairs, read Gladstone Road.

99. Car No. 42 in its original condition, unvestibuled, with saloon curtains and destinations shown on paper window stickers.

H. J. Patterson-Rutherford

Nos. 41-50. Built and supplied in 1901.

Bodies built by G. F. MILNES & Co. LTD. of Hadley, Shropshire.

Dimensions — Saloon 16′ 8″ long, 6′ 3″ wide. Overall length 27′ 8″.

Seating — 24 inside, 28 outside, total 52. 180° reversed stairs.

Electrical equipment supplied by BRITISH THOMSON-HOUSTON CO. LTD.

Two B.T-H GE.58 Motors of 35 horse power each.

Two B.T-H. B.18 controllers.

Truck — BRILL 21.E of 6 ft. wheelbase.

Braking — Hand, rheostatic and lever track brakes (as delivered).

Owing to the slow delivery of the American cars, arrangements were made for the order given to Milnes by the associated company at Chatham to be increased by ten cars and these were to be delivered to the Thanet undertaking.* They were almost identical to Chatham

*Note: It is possible that the Isle of Thanet received ten cars with single doors which had been intended for Chatham to match their Nos. 1-15, while Chatham Nos. 16-25 which had double sliding doors and were built slightly later, could have been those really intended for Thanet, where their double doors would have matched the rest of the fleet, at that time.

228

Nos. 1-15. Like them they had four windows each side with two frosted glass opening vents above each. They had narrower bodies than other cars on the Thanet system and single doors to the saloon. in which seating was on longitudinal wooden benches. Because of their narrow bodies and other constructional details they did not prove popular. As delivered, they were not vestibuled on the platforms, but after a very short time several were fitted with partial vestibules, comprising three tall panes of glass across the fronts and later others had complete vestibules with six panes of glass. Although these cars never had divided dashes like Nos. 1-40, the headlamps were on the upper deck and were moved to the dash before the war.

When No. 41 fell over the cliff at Ramsgate in 1905, it was so badly damaged that the body was stripped of all useful parts and the rest burned on the spot. Some of the parts were used to repair No. 47 damaged in another accident. After these accidents the lever track brakes with which these cars were fitted, were replaced by Spencer type track brakes, with a brass wheel on the hand brake staff.

No. 42 was converted to a one-man car in the early 1920s by the removal of the stairs and the reversal of the platform entrances; in this condition it was fully vestibuled. Soon afterwards, No. 45 was similarly converted and for the time-being both retained their upper deck appointments, although no longer accessible to passengers. Later, these were removed from No. 45 and the stair-well closed in, converting

100. Above—Car No. 42 with right-hand entrance for one-man operation, but retaining its upper deck, at the Broadstairs terminus of the "Top Road". C. Carter.

it to a single decker. From then on, it normally worked the "Top Road", taking over from No. 48, and No. 42 was kept as the relief car. At about the same time, No. 47 was fitted with fixed blade snow ploughs and appeared only in inclement weather.

No. 43 appeared in the new livery with a six window vestibule and very heavily patched dashes, otherwise most of the cars of this batch were not overhauled after the war and saw very little use. Nos. 46 & 47 were derelict in 1930 and Nos. 43, 48, 49 & 50 were stored out of use in Westbrook Depot. Only No. 44 appears to have been fully overhauled and rebuilt with a five window vestibule at each end. It took over the "Top Road" working from No. 45 in the 1930s.

Nos. 51-60. Built and supplied in 1903.

> Bodies built by — BRITISH ELECTRIC CAR CO. LTD. of Trafford Park.
>
> Dimensions — Saloon 16′ 8″ long, 6′ 6″ wide. Length over platforms 28′ 2″.
>
> Seating — 24 inside, 26 outside, total 50. 180° reversed stairs.
>
> Electrical equipment supplied by BRITISH THOMSON-HOUSTON CO. LTD.
>
> Two B.T-H. GE.58 motors of 35 horse power each.
>
> Two B.T-H. B.18 controllers.
>
> Truck — BRILL 21.E of 6′ 0″ wheelbase.
>
> Braking — Hand, rheostatic and lever track brakes (later Spencer type).

These comprised the remainder of the order through B.T-H for 20 cars, placed in 1901. They were generally similar to Nos. 41-50 but slightly wider and of typical B.E.C. construction. As supplied they had partial vestibules with two fixed windows at the front arranged in "V" formation and a band of panelling above them. Other types of screen were tried in later years, including the three and six window types used on Nos. 41-50, but most of these cars finished up with the standard five window type. Again the saloon had four side windows with two opening vents above each; there were outside-hung single sliding doors at each end, slightly offset to the near side. Wooden slatted benches were provided inside and there were plain matchboarded ceilings. They were quite fast cars and were generally regarded as

---

101. Left—Car No. 52 in its final condition at Ramsgate Harbour, showing that this batch of cars stood the years well and with the standard five window vestibules looked quite presentable.   M. J. O'Connor.
102. Centre—No. 45 in St. Peters depot yard, as cut down to a One-Man single decker.   D. W. K. Jones.
103. Right—Interior view of No. 53, showing slatted wood seats, plain ceiling and offset saloon door. Note the bulkhead windows painted black, with white notices.   D. W. K. Jones.

better than Nos. 41-50. The headlamp was moved to the dash as on the other cars and it was stated that the whole operational fleet had it in this position by 1922. Nos. 51, 52, 56 & 57 were on Brush trucks after rebuilding in the 1920s, but Nos. 53, 54, 58 & 59 remained on Brill trucks. No. 54 retained its two pane wind-screen. No. 53 was out of service in the 1920s and was probably one of the last cars to be overhauled, appearing fresh in the red livery in 1935.

Latterly Nos. 55 & 58 were out of service and No. 60 was converted for use as a Works Car. In this condition its body was not altered, but it lost its Brill truck and was mounted instead on one of the old St. Louis trucks from the 1-20 batch. It was then used for rail grinding and other similar purposes. Other cars of this batch were in regular use to the end.

No. 61. Works Car. Possibly built in own works at an early date.

Dimensions — Body 16′ 0″. Overall length 24′ 0″.

Electrical Equipment supplied by BRITISH THOMSON-HOUSTON CO. LTD.

Two B.T-H. GE.58 motors of 35 horse power each.

Two B.T-H. B.18 controllers.

Truck — BRUSH "Aa".

Braking — Hand, rheostatic and Spencer track brakes.

This was a home-made or much rebuilt vehicle used for watering, sweeping and rail grinding. The dash was quite flat with the headlamp near the bottom and to it was fixed a rather primitive windscreen with two panes of glass. A water tank was mounted between the short platforms. This came to waist height but there were full height bulkheads supporting a slightly curved roof. The trolley-mast was mounted on the tank and protruded through the roof. The body was slightly raised above the truck on timber baulks and angle-iron steps provided access to the platforms.

The car was painted maroon, with cream side pillars and vestibule window frames. It was lined in yellow with the title "Thanet Tramways" on the tank-side and the number 61 on the dash. Latterly it was painted plain grey and from 1928 it stood alongside St. Peters Depot in a very derelict condition, its duties having been taken over by No. 60.

There was also a high sided railway type goods truck, unnumbered, with a wheel operated screwdown hand-brake at one end.

Destination equipment

At first the cars only had paper stickers fixed to the two centre saloon windows, but before very long black enamelled iron plates

The Service Vehicles

104. Upper—No. 61 the works car in its condition as in the 1920s at St. Peters, with the open goods truck beside it.

C. Carter.

105. Lower—Car No. 60 as converted to a works car and mounted on a St. Louis truck, almost concealing the now derelict No. 61.

D. W. K. Jones.

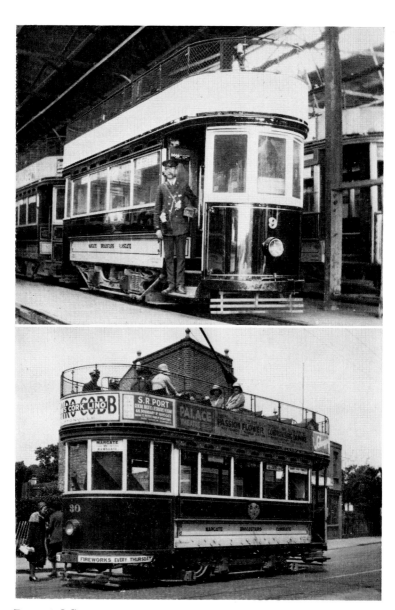

Renovated Cars.

106. Upper—No. 9 in the depot, evidently one of the first post-war overhauls, without coat of arms and retaining its St. Louis truck and original vestibule.   D. W. K. Jones.

107. Lower—No. 30 at Ramsgate in its final condition. Note the half window at near end of saloon.   Late Dr. Hugh Nicol.

with white lettering were hung on the dash; in the case of Nos. 1-40, they were placed on the lower panel, so as not to obscure the car's number. They read:—

For the Main Line:—

MARGATE

ST. PETERS BROADSTAIRS

RAMSGATE

For the "Top Road":—

BROADSTAIRS STATION

— & —

HARBOUR RAMSGATE

displayed thus at one end of the car and the names in reverse order at the other end. When on short workings between Broadstairs and Ramsgate Harbour, via Broadstairs sea front, cars carried the second board, with a sticker reading "Broadstairs Front". Subsequently boards bearing destinations were carried for a time, on brackets below the saloon windows, but later they were moved to the rocker panel. However, from about 1911, the metal plates were moved to the end wire screens of the upper deck, leaving the dash free for the later positioning there of the head-lamp.

By the end of the 1914-1918 war the metal plates had disappeared and henceforth no destination indication was shown to the front. The coats of arms were painted out and the side boards were now carried on the waist panel. No. 45, as a single decker, carried a small four-sided lettered block on the end of the roof.

When the new livery was adopted in 1927, the only destination display provided, was a series of small slip boards, one above the other in the vestibule window nearest the saloon. Each showed a single name in white on red and could be turned over to display a blank reverse side. They normally showed:—

MARGATE

RAMSGATE

Via BROADSTAIRS Front

or

BROADSTAIRS STATION

RAMSGATE HARBOUR

Via TOP ROAD

When on short workings, cars also carried a board in the nearside front vestibule window, which read:—

To MARGATE

STATION Only

and presumably other descriptions as required. This board took the place at other times occupied by a Greyhound Racing panel bill.

Livery

1901-1927. Rich maroon and yellowish cream. The dash, waist panel, cantrail and truck were maroon, while the rocker panel, window frames, stair stringers and upper deck panelling were cream. The maroon parts were lined out in gold, with at first, most elaborate scrollwork designs at the end of the waist panel. Although the dashes of Nos. 1-40 were divided into two panels, each lined out separately, both were maroon, with a gold shaded number on the upper one. The upper deck was not lined and Nos. 41-60 had the number in black beside the head-lamp thus, No. (headlamp) 45. Later the headlamp was moved to the dash as on Nos. 1-40, to allow room for advertisements. The coats of arms of the three towns served, Margate, Broadstairs and Ramsgate appeared in that order on a cream oval in the centre of the waist panel until the war years, when the lining was simplified and the coats of arms omitted. The rocker panel, at first lined in gold was then lined black. The company's motor-buses were painted in a similar livery.

Just after the war, some trams were painted green instead of maroon.

1927-1937. As cars were reconditioned, they were painted in a new and brighter livery. The maroon was replaced by light crimson red lined in yellow and the cream by off-white with black lining on the rocker panel. Both the yellow and the black lining had a fancy "V" shaped pattern in the corners. On the rocker panel there appeared the words MARGATE BROADSTAIRS RAMSGATE in black lettering; after the first few cars had been re-painted the coats of arms were reinstated on the waist panels. The number on the dash was gold shaded blue and the inside of the dash was buff. Trucks and lifeguards were in the usual oxide brown, while the trolley-mast, collision fenders, hand rails, controllers and netting round the upper deck were black. The stair stringers were red.

It was thought that, if the Company's buses had been painted in this shade of red, they would have been too similar to the East Kent buses, although slightly brighter; so a green livery was adopted for them. They were painted in a medium green, somewhat lighter than Maidstone & District, with off-white window frames and black waist bands. Like the trams, they carried the coats of arms on a cream oval.

Advertising on Cars

In the very early days, the cars did not carry external advertisements and Ramsgate Council evidently objected to them. However, after a very short time, the usual enamelled iron plates were carried on the upper deck panelling, with a curved cut-out on either side of the headlamp, as at Chatham. This did entail the transposition of the number to the dash on cars Nos. 41-60.

With the later livery and the removal of the headlamp to the dash on all cars, the more usual layout of advertisements on the canopies could be adopted, with one across the front and one on each corner: many of the cars then had "Munro Cobbs, Furnishers" in green letters on white or "Kent Messenger" in black on yellow at the ends, while the very common paper displays, such as "Whitbread's Ale & Stout" or "Black & White Whisky" appeared on the sides. Car No. 24 appeared to have had exclusive advertising for "Schweppes Mineral Waters" (white on light blue) at one stage. As the greater number of cars did not have glass opening vents above the windows, paper transparencies could not be carried in that position, but were often carried near the tops of the windows, while other notices were affixed lower down. Paper stickers, usually with red lettering on white, advertising local entertainment events, were pasted onto the collision fenders. The advertising contractor was J. W. Courtenay & Co.

Power Supply and Current Collection

Since it played so important a part in the general history of the Company, the power supply is described in the main text of this chapter.

The cars always collected their current through ordinary swivel trolley heads, some small "Bristol" type were used in later years. Bracket, span wire and centre post suspension were used, but objection was taken to the centre posts along the sea front in Margate and they had to be replaced by span-wire in 1907, but the centre posts on some of the reserved track sections remained in position throughout the life of the system. Bracket posts varied in length from quite long, to one at Westbrook which was so short that there was not even room for the simplest scrollwork on the track side of the post. Although manufactured in Ireland, the cast iron bases and ornamental scroll-work on the posts, were of quite the usual design for the period and they remained in evidence to the end. Finials were of the ball and spike design. (See page 184.)

Services and Timetables

A frequent service was always provided on the main line of the tramway, particularly during the summer months. Booklet timetables of the tram and bus services were distributed and those relating to the summers during the 1930s were got up in red covers, with the title in old English type and an advertisement for the electricity supply on the front and "Munro Cobb's" on the back. They are interesting in that one set of times was shown for the whole week, with a footnote "Times in heavy type not on Sundays." On weekdays, the first car left St. Peters at 5.30 a.m. for Westbrook and the next three cars started from Westbrook Depot in 1931, but subsequently all started out from St. Peters depot and reached Westbrook slightly later. There was an approximately 20 minute service until 9.30 a.m. and then a 10 minute service until 11.30 after which it was "every few minutes" until 9.0 p.m., (i.e. every 6 minutes in summer 12 in winter) when the evening breakdown began and several cars terminated at Ramsgate Harbour instead of going right up to the station.

The "Top Road" route had an hourly service, from 10.15 a.m. to 9.15 p.m. only, but some cars ran into service at Ramsgate via the top road and there were some short workings between Broadstairs Station and Ramsgate Harbour, via Broadstairs Front and some to Margate Station only.

The centre page spread of the booklet contained a map of the area, showing bus and tram routes overprinted in red. However it was based on an out of date Ordnance map, showing the railway stations in their positions before 1926!

(Please see Appendix "I" for list of motor-bus routes operated by the Thanet Company between 1928 and 1937).

In October 1936, not long before they took over the Thanet tram and bus services, the East Kent Company adopted route numbers, so that in due course the Thanet services were renumbered 49/A (tram service), 51, 52, 56, 54/A, 55, 53, 57, 72 and 63 (Thanet bus routes 1-8 & 10).

It will be noted that apart from route 3 becoming 57 and 6 becoming 53, they followed a fairly logical sequence. Later a new route 50 followed part of the tram service and numerous other changes have taken place in the years that have followed, particularly because of the mass evacuation of the area during the war and the changes in urban development which have taken place subsequently.

Forty nine vehicles from the Thanet bus fleet were taken over by East Kent and retained by them. They were soon repainted in the East Kent crimson and buff livery and renumbered between 1031 and 1079 (not in the same order as their Thanet numbers). (See appendix "H".) The new covered top Daimlers remained in service until after the war, when at least one was converted to an open topper for summer or tree-cutting use.

Fares and Tickets

The Light Railway Order covering the inauguration of the Thanet system fixed the fares at one penny per mile, with a maximum fare of sixpence which covered a route mileage of $11\frac{1}{2}$ miles.

Apart from this note, there exists no record of early faretables other than the Bell Punch tickets seen in various collections, all of which were of the full geographical style.

From these, it would seem that the scale of one penny per mile was not rigidly adhered to, especially in the higher values, as a fivepenny value has been seen bearing the following farestages only:— "S.E.R. Station, Ramsgate to Margate terminus".

Evidently the original scale of fares did not provide the revenue required to meet all eventualities, and a new scale of fares was introduced in April, 1911, including a penny fare from Broadstairs Front to St. Peters. The throughout fare was then raised from 5d. to 6d., for which a ticket coloured dark cerise has been seen.

In the late 1920s, the tramway company commenced the issue of a timetable book which also contained faretables for both trams and buses. By this time the throughout fare on the tram route was 7d.

---

106. Opposite—A selection of Thanet tickets, loaned by R. J. Durrant, N. D. W. Elston and the Omnibus Society.

Photographed by A. D. Packer.

Single: 10d. Return, and from comparison of this faretable dated July 1931 with the early tickets seen, it would seem that the main effect of First War increases was the shortening of intermediate fare-stages thus raising the higher fares. A peculiarity of the 1931 fare-table was the absence of twopenny adult fares, the scale going straight from $1\frac{1}{2}$d. to $2\frac{1}{2}$d.

Workmen's tickets have been seen, ranging from $1\frac{1}{2}$d to $7\frac{1}{2}$d. in $1\frac{1}{2}$d. steps.

Children under five years of age were carried free if seated on the passengers lap, whilst all children occupying seats, or over five years of age were charged the full adult fare. Dogs were charged for at one penny per journey, and had to be kept on a lead and not allowed to roam round the car.

Parcels were charged for at one penny per trip, but, according to the timetable, this charge only applied to luggage and bulky parcels weighing over 28 lbs. Examination of the faretable for July 1936 reveals that the throughout fare had been reduced to 6d. Single, with the return fare remaining at 10d. Twopenny adult fares had been inserted in the chart as follows:—

Pegwell Road, Ramsgate to Broadstairs Front.

Broadstairs Front and St. Peters Tram Depot.

Broadstairs Broadway and Victoria Avenue (Northdown).

Church Street (St. Peters) and Northdown Corner.

There was also a local twopenny fare in Margate between Athelstan Road and Westonville Garage. Another new fare value hitherto unseen in the scale was $5\frac{1}{2}$d., Single, of which there were five instances, as follows:—

Ramsgate Terminus to St. Peters (Tram Depot).

Pegwell Road, Ramsgate to Victoria Avenue (Northdown).

Paragon Corner to The Wheatsheaf.

Broadstairs Front to Margate Station.

Broadstairs Broadway to Westbrook Terminus.

To turn to the tickets themselves, as stated in a previous paragraph the early issues were of the fully geographical style, the full extent of the stage covered being set in separated boxes either side of a central column containing the fare value, together with the words "Issued subject to the Company's Bye-laws". The title of the company was given as "The Isle of Thanet Electric Tramways Co., Ltd.", the printer being the Bell Punch Company, Ltd.

In common with other tramway authorities, the Thanet tramways suffered sundry adjustments to the fares in the period just after the first World War, and towards the end of operation, and which often necessitated frequent changes to the printed matter, particularly fare-stage names. In order to lower printing costs it was decided to introduce the style of ticket known to the trade as "deaf and dumb" as numbers were used to denote farestages instead of geographical definitions.

In London, where this system was used by the smaller municipal systems, each stage was given a number in numerical order from one end of the route to the other, but, on the Thanet system, a penny ticket punched at Stage 1, indicated that it was available between Ramsgate Terminus and Pegwell Road. There were 14 one penny stages; thirteen at 1½d. and 2½d.; ten at 3d.; seven at 4d. and 5d.; 3 at 6d. and one at 7d. An unusual feature of the tickets was the fact that both 1d. and 1½d., values were printed on white paper with the printed matter on the penny value done in black, whilst the 1½d value was printed in red. Investigation of the clippings retained in the Bell Punch would always provide a check should there be any query as to the number of tickets of each value sold.

Return tickets were withdrawn on the second journey and an Exchange ticket, coloured green, issued in their place. There were not separate Exchange tickets for each value of return ticket issued, of which there were four (4½d., 6d., 8d. and 10d.). These were shown in the faretables as follows:—

4½d. Return *(Stage number in brackets)*: —
(1) Broadstairs Broadway to Ramsgate Harbour.

6d. Return *(Stage numbers in brackets)*: —
(1) York Street, Ramsgate to Church Street, St. Peters.
(2) Broadstairs Broadway to Margate Station.

8d. Return *(Stage number in brackets)*: —
(1) Broadstairs Front to Margate Station.

10d. Return *(Stage number in brackets)*: —
(1) Ramsgate Terminus to Westbrook Terminus.

It will be seen from this list of return fares that Stage No. 1 on the Exchange ticket could refer to four differing farestage points in either direction, which could lead to confusion for a ticket inspector, as the return tickets were not of the two-coupon variety, and, after an Exchange ticket had been received from the Conductor by the Passenger, the recipient had no proof of the value return ticket he had handed over. There were eight stage numbers on the Exchange Ticket, and it could well be that Stage numbers 3 to 8 were used in some special way to indicate the value of the return tendered for the Exchange Ticket.

A special ticket, coloured yellow, and priced at one penny was issued in respect of parcels, but although dogs were charged for, no special ticket has been seen. It could well be, however, that stage numbers 15 and 16 on the ordinary penny ticket and which did not apply to the faretable, were used for this purpose.

The Workmen's Returns were of the two-coupon variety, fully geographical, and on the return journey, the bottom half was retained by the conductor, the top half being punched in the stage for which it was available and handed back to the passenger, together with an Exchange ticket.

In June 1924 the title of the company was changed to "The Isle of Thanet Electric Supply Company Ltd.", and this title appeared on the tickets soon after.

By July 1936, the tramway fares and stages had been revised and the number of farestages increased from 14 to 19. This presented no problem from the ticket angle, as by this time the inserted type of Setright ticket machine had been introduced. This system used a pre-printed ticket which was inserted into the machine and the value of the fare, together with the number representing the stage at which the passenger boarded were printed on the ticket after manipulation of the various dials and handles fixed at the side of the machine. Two tickets of this type have been seen, one coloured green for Ordinary Single fares, and one coloured primrose and overprinted in red with $\frac{1}{2}$d. value, which could be used for odd fares such as $2\frac{1}{2}$d. and $3\frac{1}{2}$d. etc. On these tickets, which appear to have been printed by Colleys Ltd., the Company's title is abbreviated to "I.T.E.S. Co., Ltd.".

This brings the story of the Thanet tickets to a close.

The colours of Thanet tickets were: —

Early Geographical
Tickets:—
1d. White.
1$\frac{1}{2}$d. Salmon
2d. Red.
3d. Blue.
4d. Buff.
5d. Green.
6d. Dark Red.

Parcels Tickets:—
1d. Yellow.

Workman's Returns:—
1$\frac{1}{2}$d., 3d., 4$\frac{1}{2}$d., 6d., 7$\frac{1}{2}$d. All coloured flame.

Later Numerical
Tickets:—
1d. White (text in black).
1$\frac{1}{2}$d. „ (text in red).
2$\frac{1}{2}$d. Orange.
3d. Red.
4d. Blue.   6d. Buff.
4$\frac{1}{2}$d. Blue.   7$\frac{1}{2}$d. Green.
5d. Green.   9d. Flame.

Ordinary Returns:—
4$\frac{1}{2}$d. Brown.
6d. Grey.
8d. Primrose.
10d. Magenta.

Exchange Tickets:— Two types have been seen, both coloured green. An early one had a red skeleton overprint "E" with red hatching along each side, whilst the later one carried neither overprint or hatching.

CHAPTER SIX

THE FOLKESTONE, SANDGATE AND HYTHE TRAMWAYS COMPANY
Also
PIER TRAMWAYS, CLIFF LIFTS AND MISCELLANEOUS LINES

The Folkestone, Hythe and Sandgate Tramways Company

FOLKESTONE is one of the larger and more fashionable Kentish seaside resorts; the town which is surrounded by hills up to 600 feet high, is particularly well planned. It is also a Channel Port, both the railway and the cross-channel steamers coming to Folkestone in 1843. At the Leas, the seashore is overhung by cliffs, on top of which stand some of the fashionable hotels served by a cliff lift. Cheriton and Shorncliffe lie on the high ground to the north-west. The latter is best known for Shorncliffe Camp, now a permanent barracks but first used by Sir John Moore, when training troops for the assault of Coruña in 1794. Below the Shorncliffe Heights lies Sandgate, which has developed as a small seaside resort over the last 100 years. Although formerly separate municipal entities, Cheriton and Sandgate now form part of the Borough of Folkestone (as in 1970).

Slightly further to the west lies Hythe, once a port and mentioned in A.D. 732, but owing to the sea receding, now lies slightly inland at the foot of the hills. It is a quiet country town, but was well known during the 1914-1918 war for the Hythe School of Musketry and the nearby Royal Military Canal, which had been constructed as part of the defences against Napoleon. More recently, Hythe had become better known as the eastern terminus of the Romney, Hythe and Dymchurch Railway, a miniature line opened in 1927. (Like the tramway named in the title above, it shunned a true geographical order in the names quoted in its title).

The Hythe and Sandgate branch of the South Eastern Railway although authorized in 1864, was not opened until 9th October 1874; the line started at Sandling Junction and was $3\frac{1}{2}$ miles in length. Powers were sought in 1876 for a further extension from Sandgate to Folkestone Harbour, using what later became part of the horse tramway as an alternative to the very steeply graded Folkestone Junction-Folkestone Harbour line which exists today. Under public pressure the application was withdrawn.

The possibility of serving the area by trams was first considered in 1880, when a Bill entitled the "Folkestone, Sandgate and Hythe

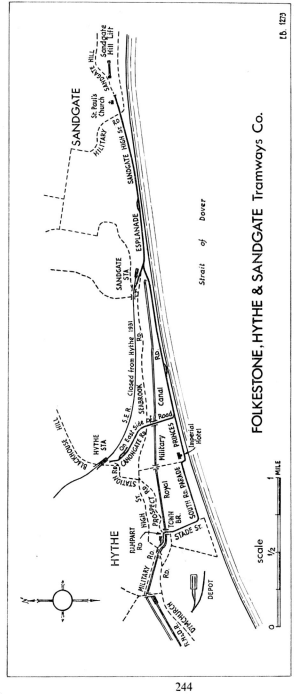

FOLKESTONE, HYTHE & SANDGATE Tramways Co.

108. Map of the Sandgate & Hythe Tramway.   E. Beddard.

Tramway" was placed before Parliament by Henry Davey and E. E. Allen. The ensuing Order empowered a company of that name to build a tram line of 3 ft. 6 in. gauge, 2¾ miles in length from Sandgate Road at Albion Terrace to a point near the bridge over the Seabrook Stream in Hythe. For the purpose of the Bill, it was set out as twenty "Tramways", each passing loop and intervening section of single track being described separately. Thus there would have been ten loops, but this scheme was not proceeded with. It has been remarked that "never did so small a tramway obtain so many parliamentary powers". No doubt this was in reference to the habit in these early days of dividing proposals up into many separate "Tramways" when applying to Parliament. However, further Bills were deposited in 1884, 1886, 1888, 1892 and 1900.

The first of these was passed as the "Folkestone, Sandgate and Hythe Tramways Act" on 28th July 1884, again authorizing the incorporation of a company bearing that title, which was empowered to construct a standard gauge tramway to be worked by animal traction only, but which could come to a working agreement with the South Eastern Railway Company, permitting the latter to work, use, manage and maintain the tramway. Two years were allowed for its construction and temporary tramways could be laid down, but work was not to proceed between 1st June and 31st October. The tramway was to grant workmen's fares and its capital was set at £15,000.

Of the several tramways proposed in the Bill, only the following two were approved:—

Tramway No. 4.   2 miles 0 furlongs 526 yards of single line and 308 yards of double line.

Commencing in the Esplanade, Sandgate at the termination of Tramway No. 3, 67 yards west of Bathing Establishment and proceeding along the Hythe and Sandgate road to Twiss Road at a point south of the Royal Military Canal.

Tramway No. 4A.   160 yards of single line and 44 yards of double line.

Commencing by a junction with Tramway No. 4 on Hythe & Sandgate road 83 yards east of the Lifeboat House and proceeding by Sandgate Station Approach road to the western end thereof.

Evidently Tramways Nos. 1, 2 and 3 would have been extensions from Sandgate in the direction of Folkestone (no doubt turned down because they were too steep for animal traction and because of local opposition). Tramway No. 4 above would have kept to the Hythe-Sandgate road throughout, instead of Princes Road over which it was eventually constructed.

The Bill promoted in 1886, sought an extension of time and powers

245

to abandon certain tramways approved in the 1884 Act, but to build others in their place. The section to be abandoned comprised 83 yards east of the Lifeboat House at Seabrook. The additional sections were:—

Tramway No. 1.	6 furlongs 8.50 chains single line.
	Commencing in the approach road to Hythe Station (S.E.R.), crossing the Hythe and Sandgate road, passing over the Royal Military Canal and terminating on the north-west side of Princes Road opposite the eastern end of Seabrook Hotel.
Tramway No. 2.	1 mile 0 furlongs 8.86 chains single line.
	Commencing in Princes Road at the termination of Tramway No. 1 and passing along Princes Road, Hythe and Sandgate Road to the termination of Tramways Nos. 1 & 2 of the 1884 Bill.
Tramway No. 3.	4 furlongs 1.25 chains single line and 1.75 chains double line.
	Commencing at a junction with Tramway No. 1 of the 1884 Bill at 67 yards west of the entrance to Sandgate Bathing Establishment and passing along the Broadway or High Street, Sandgate to the National School.

Additional crossing places were permitted where necessary and animal or mechanical traction could be used, including electricity. The South Eastern Railway Company were permitted to contribute up to £1,000 of the Company's capital. In connection with this, the railway company obtained an Act of Parliament itself on 12th July 1887 permitting it to guarantee the interest on the tramway company's capital. Another Bill presented by the tramway interests in 1888 sought a further extension of time to 31st May 1889 and power to alter the gauge to 3 ft. 6 in. Steam traction was also mentioned therein.

Yet another Bill was presented in 1892; this did not relate to the provision of street tramways, but to a lift to be owned by the tramway company and to link the West Lawn, Cheriton* with Shorncliffe Camp. Its length was to be 18 chains and the gauge to be 4ft. 8 in. (sic). Any power other than animal could be used and three years were allowed for completion. The maximum toll was to be 3d per person. However, this project came to nothing.

*It is suggested that Sandgate was really intended here.

109. Top—The saloon car No. 1 near the depot in Hythe.
Courtesy E. Harrison.
110. Centre—Open toastrack car No. 5 on Princes Parade near the Seabrook Hotel. Courtesy J. H. Price.
111. Bottom—One of the covered cross-bench cars on the passing loop in Princes Parade. Note smart uniforms of the driver & conductor, also well fed horses. Courtesy W. A. Camwell.

112. Upper—No. 5 again, this time at the Sandgate terminus, about to depart for Hythe.   H. J. Patterson-Rutherford.
113. Lower—Covered car No. 4 waits at Sandgate terminus while the horses are walked round.   Courtesy J. H. Price.

Construction and Opening

The first part of what was to become the tramway, was in fact built as a long railway siding in Canongate Road, Hythe, starting from the Railway Station and extending to and along the sea front. It was used for the construction of Princes Parade, laid out by Sir John Goode as part of a grandiose scheme for Sir Edward Watkin, Chairman of the South Eastern Railway. He was always interested in promoting housing and town planning schemes around the railways which he controlled, notably the Metropolitan Railway and this was his contribution to the South Eastern. Although the contractor's line was at first worked by horse-drawn wagons, before long they acquired a steam locomotive which had worked on the Berber-Suakim Railway in the Anglo-Egyptian Sudan. (Mr. Lee's recent researches show that the latter was originally laid to standard gauge and consequently the locomotive was not of the 3 ft. 6 in. gauge as previously suggested). Princes Parade was officially opened by the Prince of Wales in 1883.

Although construction commenced on the tramway extending towards Sandgate in 1889, it was halted at the Coast Guard Station in May, because of Lord Radnor's objections. He wanted the gauge to be 3 ft. 6 in. and the use of steam power was discussed.

It was some time before the construction work recommenced towards Sandgate, but the tramway line when extended in the other direction incorporated that part of the railway siding which ran along Princes Parade. The section in Canongate Road was never used for passenger traffic and later became derelict. The first part of the passenger line was completed and ran from Sandgate School to the Seabrook Hotel (now the Imperial Hotel), via Sandgate High Street, the Esplanade, the Promenade and Princes Parade, Seabrook. The latter was not made up and the tram track was laid on what was in fact a semi-private right of way. There was a loop on this section on which right-hand running was observed, so that the cars got a straight run through the points when entering the loop. At the several paths leading to bridges across the Hythe Canal, there were white painted notice boards, giving lists of fares and other useful information. The first section of the tramway was opened on 18th May 1891, presumably after the usual Board of Trade Inspection, but there is no surviving record of an opening ceremony.

Construction continued on the remaining section of the line to Hythe and this was opened on 6th June 1892. It ran via South Road, Stade Street and Rampart Road, terminating in Red Lion Square, where there was subsequently a trailing connection into the depot, behind which were the stables, since the line was worked by horses. On this section, there were some quite sharp curves and the cars were equipped with water tanks on the platforms, with taps which could be turned on to lubricate the wheels of the cars when they took the curves.

Although local postcards proclaimed "By toastrack — four miles by the sea", the line was in fact 3 miles 29 chains in length, laid to standard gauge with two passing loops. Five cars were provided, one of which was a closed saloon, two were roofed cross-bench cars and two were open cross-bench cars. However, it appears that when the winter service was given up in later years, the saloon car was rebuilt as another crossbench car. Each car was pulled by two horses, of which there were twenty five on the strength.

The Route Described

The line started near the foot of Sandgate Hill, close to Sandgate School. It ran along the narrow High Street lined with shops and some ancient timber faced houses as far as the Coastguard Station, where the road opened out onto the sea front becoming the Esplanade, with hotels and boarding houses against the slopes behind on the right. The tram line was on the seaward side of the road here. The road continued thus for some little distance until it forked, with the main road to Hythe on the right; this was followed for a few yards by a connecting tram line, which ran up the slope to Sandgate Station. The other road to the left, which was followed by the main tram line, crossed over the Canal near its mouth, by a small bridge and carried on along the Promenade, beside the sea. Along this section, even today, there is no building, but a golf course which allows a commanding view of the hills inland. The sea front continues as Princes Parade, which as recounted earlier, remained unmade for very many years. After passing in front of the large and imposing Seabrook Hotel, the line took a right and left turn at Twiss Road into South Road, running behind the sea front, then right again into the tree-lined Stade Street and across a bridge over the Military Canal into Hythe, where the line turned left along Rampart Road into Red Lion Square, terminating in front of the Red Lion Hotel. The depot with its timbered front (now a Café) stands at the southeastern corner of the square.

Taken over by the Railway

As previously mentioned, the South Eastern Railway Company already had a certain financial interest in the tramway, no doubt through Sir Edward Watkin's real estate dealings and this may have been connected in some way with his interest in acquiring a working site for his Channel Tunnel project. On 29th June 1893, the South Eastern Railway obtained an Act of Parliament, enabling them to take the tramway over completely at a capital cost of £26,753. After this the staff were fitted out with railway guard type uniforms. A twenty minute service continued to be provided in the summer months and a half hourly service in the winter. The single through fare was 3 pence. The depot and stable building at Hythe must have been erected after the railway company took over, since the stonework above the entrance was (and still is) lettered:—

S.E.R.

Folkestone, Hythe & Sandgate Tramways,

1894

This appears on the front of the brick building, behind the smaller timbered one. Consequently the cars must have been shedded and the horses stabled elsewhere at the beginning, certainly before the line reached Hythe. Note the changed order of place names in the

114. Upper—Open car drawn by mules, just after the 1914/18 war, on the sea front at Sandgate. Pamlin Prints.

115. Lower—Covered car with mules making its way along Princes Parade, Seabrook. H. J. Patterson-Rutherford.

title as now adopted under railway control. It has also been said that the depot would accommodate only four cars, but the stock at any one time was always five cars. There was a physical connection between the tram and the railway at Sandgate Station (actually in Seabrook), by which cars could be transferred onto the railway and taken to Ashford Works for overhaul; it has also been stated that they were sent in rotation and there was always one car at Ashford. Later, the connecting spur at Sandgate Station appears to have been

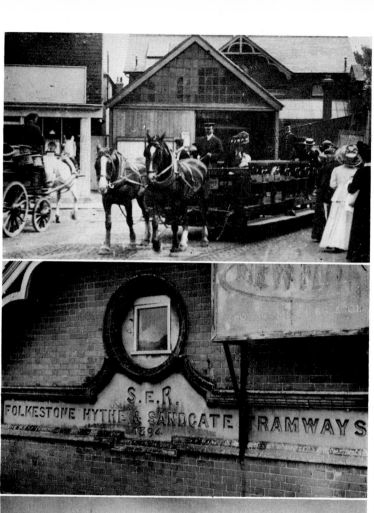

used to transport the materials used in the construction of Sandgate Hill funicular railway in 1892, as its lower station was close to the tram terminus. The cars used on it were pulled over the tramway by a team of horses. The roads parallel with the funicular were of course too steep for horse trams and this is one of the reasons why the F.H. & S. tramway was never extended into Folkestone. Moreover the various Local Authorities in the area held tramway powers (these are dealt with more fully in Chapter 8), It suffices to say here that Folkestone Corporation and Sandgate U.D.C. regarded any proposals to extend the horse tramway as an attempt to baulk their own plans.

Late in 1905, the National Electric Construction Co. Ltd., who had well advanced plans for electric tramways in Folkestone, proposed to take over the Sandgate-Hythe line and electrify it, but the local authorities objected to the use of overhead wires, particularly in Folkestone. Later Hythe Council attempted to put an increase on the rates to meet the cost incurred in 1908 for opposing the Bill, but were told in 1910, that it was illegal to do this retrospectively in respect of an expense incurred outside the current rating period.

The British Electric Traction Co. also had plans for tramways in this area. It is stated that Stephen Sellon, who represented them (see also Maidstone Chapter), hinted in January 1906 at very substantial payments for road works which would be made to the Local Authorities if the scheme were approved for a tramway from Folkestone to New Romney. Then, on 27th January 1906, Sandgate U.D.C. gave notice of its intention to acquire the section of the horse tramway which lay within its boundaries, for the purpose of electrification. Th fact that the tramway had been constructed under the 1870 Act empowered them to do this, but the threat was not followed up.

Without access to Folkestone, the only important town in the area, the tramway had very little real hope of success: competition from horse brakes began to be felt and in 1903, there had started up a service of large open motor-cars belonging to the Folkestone Motors Ltd., which charged 4d from Folkestone to Sandgate, 6d from Folkestone to Seabrook and 8d to Hythe. The higher fare than the tram was offset by the benefit of a through ride. Nevertheless, the N.E.C.'s Folkestone, Sandgate and Hythe Tramways Act of 1906, permitting the setting up of a new company, bearing that title (place names in geographical order), was presented on 4th August 1906. It

---

116. Top—No. 5 once more, in front of the depot at Hythe. The front part of the building is now a café.
117. Centre—A close up of the facade of the depot at Hythe, showing the order of place names as favoured by the South Eastern Railway.
Ray Warner.
118. Lower—No. 1 rebuilt as a covered crossbench car drawn by mules, after the war. The driver is not in uniform.
Courtesy Tramway Museum Society.

envisaged taking the tramway over from the railway company and electrifying it on the Dolter Surface Contact system, but after experiencing difficulties with their tramways at Torquay and Mexborough which already employed the Dolter system, the N.E.C. had second thoughts and made fresh proposals for the Folkestone area involving the use of overhead wires; these were rejected in 1908. (See also Chapter 8).

The War and Closing Years

With the outbreak of war, the horses were requisitioned and the service was suspended for "The Duration" on 7th August 1914. Thus, the line remained out of use throughout the war, but perhaps surprisingly, a tram service was reinstated at Whitsun 1919 (Whit Monday was 9th June), and ran during the summer months. However, horses were difficult to come by and ex-army mules were acquired instead, but this brought a number of difficulties: it is said "Their passage was erratic and they not only stopped at the wrong places, but often insisted on going in the wrong direction and round into the wrong street." Consequently, they were replaced by horses as soon as possible. The staff were no longer provided with uniforms and some women conductors were employed. There was no winter service, but the cars operated during the summers of 1919, 1920 and 1921, when the service ceased for the winter on Friday 30th September.

It was stated that many people had taken advantage of this pleasant ride by the sea. However things were going on behind the scenes and at a meeting of the Sandgate Urban District Council, held on 13th December, a formal complaint was made about the condition of the tram track and the Clerk to the Council stated that although the Act did not compel the Railway Company to run the trams, it did require them to keep the track safe for other traffic. After correspondence and a further formal complaint that work had not yet started, a site meeting was arranged between the Council Surveyor and Mr. Shaw, the District Engineer of the S.E. & C. Railway. At the next meeting of the Council on 7th February 1922, the Chairman reported that he and the Surveyor had suggested to the Railway Company that the tramway should cease running and the track be taken up. Presumably the receipts from the tramway had not been sufficient to justify the cost of repair that the Council were now demanding and it was announced that the tramway would not reopen for the coming summer season.

Thus, Friday 30th September 1921 was in fact the date of final closure. The Council decided to replace the tram track with Kentish ragstone at the expense of the railway company. However, the Railway, determined to get the last word in, wrote a letter to the Council, which was read at the meeting of 25th April 1922, asking if, before they applied for an Abandonment Order the Council would wish to exercise their option under the Tramways Act of 1870 and take over so much of the tramway as lay within their territory and work it themselves. Needless to say, the Council replied that they were not interested and reminded the Railway Company that they would be liable for the cost of reinstatement, plus 10% Establishment Charges and a surveyor's fee. At a later meeting of the Council, a member pressed for the track lifting work to be halted for the summer months, so as not to interfere with holiday traffic. Evidently this suggestion was thought to be pushing the railway company too far and was not accepted.

Now, apart from the depot buildings and stables at Hythe, used as a Café, but with the title still on the stonework above and some rails under the mat in the doorway, there is little to show that the area was ever served by a tramway; and to obliterate its memory even further, the Hythe-Sandgate section of the railway branch closed on 1st April 1931 and an East Kent bus garage was built on the site of Sandgate Station. Next, Hythe Station was closed as a wartime measure on 3rd May 1943 and re-opened on 1st October 1945. However, the branch line from Sandling Junction closed completely and for good on 3rd December 1951 and the track has since been lifted. Both Hythe and Sandgate Stations stood on the hillside above the places after which they were named.

Trackwork

Ordinary grooved tram rails were used on the sections of tram track laid on paved public roads, but railway type bullhead rails fixed by chairs to sleepers were used on the semi-private track section in Princes Parade.

Rolling Stock

Five cars were originally built for the line, one of which was subsequently rebodied. Each was drawn by two horses and had the hand-brake staff on the outside of the dash. The stock was as follows:-

(a). *No. 1 Closed Saloon for winter use.*

This had eight windows each side with curved tops, two opening on drop sashes. The roof was almost flat and the bulkheads match-boarded. Seating inside was on longitudinal benches and there were short open platforms. Delivered in May 1889, this car was of unusual appearance and is said to have been built by a London coachbuilder. When the winter service was given up, it was rebuilt in 1919 as a roofed crossbench car, similar to No. 4 but with one less bay, seating 40 passengers.

(b). *Nos. 2 & 4 Roofed crossbench cars.*

These had seating right across the car in six bays and were open at the sides, with canvas curtains which could be drawn down in inclement weather. There were open platforms and glazed bulkheads. They seated 45 passengers.

(c). *Nos. 3 & 5 Open crossbench cars.*

These also had seating right across the car in six bays and open sides. There were open platforms but no bulkhead or roof. They were for settled summer weather.

Livery

The cars were painted all over in one colour, South Eastern Carriage Lake. The saloon car was lined out in gold, with patterns in the corners. The other cars had similar lining on the dash only. The number appeared in small figures in one corner of the dash, with at one time "S.E.R." in the opposite corner. Had the number been placed in the more usual central position, it would have been obscured by the horse's posterior. The covered cars carried roof boards, apparently in the main body colour, with wording in gold shaded letters. They read:—

"Sandgate to Sea View Bridge — Fare 2d" "Sea View Bridge to Hythe — Fare 2d". Above the saloon windows on the enclosed car and on a separate board on Nos. 2 & 4, was another inscription:—

"S.E. & C.R. Sandgate, Hotel Imperial & Hythe — Fare 3d".

Fares & Tickets

The original through fare was probably 4d, but after the line was taken over by the railway, fares were as described on the route boards mentioned above. In later years the fare was 6d from end to end. Tickets were on traditional coloured card. A green 1d. ticket with named stages has been seen, and a 6d. ticket (colour not recorded).

119. Above—The only known specimens of Hythe & Sandgate tickets and an example of the tickets in use on cliff lifts, this one from Margate.
Photographed by A. D. Packer & Ray Warner.

120. Opposite—Looking down Sandgate Hill lift, below the loop, showing the two inner rails close together.
Courtesy Eric Harrison.

CLIFF RAILWAYS

The Kent coast is largely bounded by steep cliffs and consequently there have been built a number of cliff lifts and inclined railways at the more populous resorts.

(a) In the Folkestone Area
1. Sandgate Hill Lift.

As already mentioned, the lower terminus of this line was only a short distance from the Sandgate terminus of the horse tramway. It was owned by the Sandgate Hill Lift Company Ltd., incorporated on 21st April 1892. The materials for its construction were brought by rail to Sandgate Station, thence over the horse tramway to just below the lower station. The line was completed and opened during February 1893. It was 670 feet 6 inches in length, running almost parallel to the coast, with a track gauge of 5 ft. 6 in. There was a passing place at the mid point, but the rest was laid with four rails, the inner ones being so close together that cars could not pass. The gradient of the incline was variable and part of the line was on an embankment to allow sufficient headroom to cross over the road on a bridge at Radnor Cliff Crescent. Thus there was a gradient of 1 in 4.75 at each end and 1 in 7.04 over the central section of 267 ft. 6 in. Part of the line was in a wooded cutting.

There were two cars of tramway type with clerestory roofs, mounted on triangular underframes, attached to opposite ends of a cable running on pulleys between the rails. Each car which accommodated 16 persons and could carry bath chairs, kept to its own track and they

257

121. Folkestone Metropole Lift.   Cross's Library, Folkestone.

were operated on the hydraulic counterbalance system. It was therefore a true funicular, rather than a lift. Speed was limited to 4 m.p.h., and the cars were fitted with hand brakes and automatic wedge track brakes to prevent them from running back.

The line fell on evil days during the 1914-1918 war and was finally closed in July 1918. Rehabilitation was considered, but the owning company went into liquidation in June 1923, after which the tramway was dismantled and the terminal buildings were converted into dwelling houses, but the piers at Radnor Cliff Crescent, which had supported the bridge, were very strongly constructed and are still in position. The author H. G. Wells once lived in Spade House adjoining the western abutment.

2. Folkestone Metropole Lift

The Folkestone Metropole Lift Company Ltd. was incorporated on 12th May 1903 and the line was opened on 31st March 1904. It was a short water-balanced inclined lift joining the Lower Sandgate Road with the Leas, close to the Metropole Hotel and the Grand Hotel, being intended primarily for the patrons of the former, but it was also available to the general public at a fare of 2d. It had a regular inclination and sea water was used as ballast in the descending car, being pumped back to a storage tank at the top, by two Crossley gas engine pumping units located in the lower station.

The railway was closed in 1939 on the outbreak of the second world war and was allowed to fall into disrepair. In 1950 one car was described as being completely enveloped in undergrowth and no effort was made to rehabilitate the line. It was dismantled in 1951.

3. Folkestone Cliff Lift

This lift is located at the eastern end of the Leas and used to belong to the Folkestone Passenger Lift Company Ltd. incorporated on 13th June 1885, under the Folkestone Pier and Lift Act of 1884. It was first opened to the public on 16th September of that year in time for the regatta, having been inspected by Major General Hutchinson on 11th, but was opened officially on 21st September 1885. The lower terminus was opposite Langford Terrace. The gauge adopted was 5 ft. 10 in. and the length 145 ft. The engineer in charge of its construction was John Collins, who was also responsible for the other two lines already described. Evidently traffic more than came up to expectations, to such an extent that in 1890, a second pair of tracks was installed alongside the existing ones. Strangely enough, these were not of the same gauge as the original pair, but were 5 ft. 8½ in. The railway was operated on the water balance system and was equipped by Messrs. Waygood & Co., of London, predecessors of the present Waygood, Otis Co. Ltd. The capital cost of the installation was £2,957.

The original pair of cars have stepped floors, 7 entrances and staggered windows, but the later pair have tram-car type bodies with level floors and are mounted on triangular underframes. The stepped floor cars seat 14 and the others 16.

This pair of installations survived the two wars and in October 1967, was taken over by the Corporation who still operate it. A flag is flown from the top station when a service is operating. It runs in a pleasant setting among trees and the lower station building is quite

122. Folkestone Cliff Lift in 1954.   Photo J. H. Price.

attractive. At the top there are just gates and steps up to the promenade.

In June 1963, there was an accident which caused a good deal of comment in the local press. One of the cars failed to slow up when it approached the lower station and hit the buffer stop rather violently. Two soldiers who were travelling in the lift at the time, held down some children and prevented them from being injured by the impact and flying glass. They were Sergeant Major D. Hurst and Sergeant B. Davies, both of whom received the Queen's Commendation for Brave Conduct. The pair of lifts with the stepped floors has not been in use of recent years having worked last on 27th October 1966. Whether this has any connection with the accident described above, is not known. Both cars are parked in the bottom station.

The two cars with flat floors continue to provide a service in the summer months and are painted pale yellow (formerly dark brown & white).

Fares were formerly collected at turnstiles, but after the Corporation took over, an "Ultimate" ticket issuing machine was installed in the lower station, where all fares are now collected.

(b). **The Thanet Area.**

4. **Viking Bay Lift — Broadstairs**

This lift which connects the top of the cliff with the sands has its lower terminus at Viking Bay and its upper terminus adjoining Albion Street, Broadstairs. Like the last mentioned line, it was installed by Waygood & Co. Ltd. and had a single 12 passenger car running on a single track in a sloping tunnel, cut through a chalk cliff 100 feet high. The car is cable hauled and operated by an electric motor. Its track gauge is 5 ft. 3 in. It was opened in 1910 and the original owner was a Mr. Graham Tucker, but at some time in the early days it was under the same ownership as the vertical lifts at Ramsgate (see No. 6 below); it is believed to be now owned by a Mr. F. J. Langrebe.

The lift is still in use in the summer months and tickets are not given for fares taken except that large card season tickets are available.

5. **Margate-Cliftonville Lido Lift**

All the lifts so far described climb away from the sea directly against or cut into a sloping cliff face. This one differs in that it runs sideways at 45° against a brick retaining wall supporting a vertical cliff face. It was installed in 1912/13, again by Messrs Waygood Otis Ltd. for the owners who at the time were probably the same as No. 4. above. It is at present owned by the Margate Estate Co. Ltd. who also own the well known Dreamland Amusement Park, with a 15 inch gauge miniature railway of long standing, opened in 1924 with 2 steam and 1 petrol locomotive. They also own a miniature railway on Margate Jetty of 10¼ inch gauge, 1 locomotive. Both railways use T.I.M. tickets issued from a machine carried by the driver.

The top of the lift is opposite Athelstan Road, where the trams ran and is electrically operated, with an iron counterbalance weight, which descends in a vertical shaft. The motor runs at 480 volts D.C. and produces 15 horse power. There is one metal bodied car with a rounded roof, which was rebuilt and slightly modified in 1947, since when it has been painted red. The track gauge is 5 feet and the line is still in operation in the summer months with a travelling attendant who collects the fares (2 new pence per person, children half price) issuing Bell Punch tickets, from a roll and of a different colour for each day of the week.

Margate Corporation owns a vertical cliff lift opened in 1936, with a cabin holding 40 passengers.

6. Ramsgate Vertical Lifts

There are three ordinary vertical lifts with single cabins at Ramsgate, connecting the top of the cliff with the promenade below. The Marina Lift is on the East Cliff near the Promenade Pier and rises 68 feet in a vertical brick tower, surmounted by a cupola with the date 1908 marked on it and a weather vane. The Harbour Lift, not far away dates from 1910 and is close to the site of the former Ramsgate Harbour Station, later the terminus of the Ramsgate Tunnel Railway (see page 276). Its vertical rise is 58 feet and the car carries 20 passengers. Like the former it is enclosed in a brick tower. The third lift is of later date and rises 78 feet in a concrete shaft, located at the West Cliff.

The first two lifts were originally owned by Cliff Lifts Ltd. of Falmouth Road, London, who also owned the lifts at Broadstairs and Margate in the early days.

Originally, Williamson tickets torn from a roll were used, but later these were replaced by vertical "Automatickets" and more recently "Autoslot" machines have been installed at the upper and lower termini, from which passengers serve themselves with tickets. Roll tickets are still kept for emergency use. The original fare was 1d.

Folkestone — Lower Toll Road

While on the subject of fares and tickets, perhaps we should not pass without mention of the toll road running along the bottom of the cliff from West Folkestone towards Sandgate. There were three gates on this road, one at each end and one in the middle. Only the middle gate was used in the winter and the two end ones during the summer. Williamson tickets of vertical format were used recently, bearing the wording "Lower Road Tollgate". At different times both punch type and roll tickets have been used . The area was taken over from Lord Radnor, by the Corporation on 1st April 1973, when the outer gates were replaced by automatic parking ticket machines and the middle gate by an automatic lifting barrier, on a payment of 10p.

RAMSGATE
EAST CLIFF & SANDS LIFT

FARE 1ᴰ

A Sail down the Pier.

HERNE BAY PIER TRAMWAYS
A Sword and a Tablecloth

IF mastery of the seas is in every Briton's blood then perhaps the mainspring for that seemingly British phenomenon, the seaside pier, has been found; on them, even those whose stomachs do not live up to their aspirations can commune with the waves in peace. To carry the thought a little further, just as a ship is a self-contained world, so the Victorian pier strove to emulate it by providing food appropriate to the hour. Musical and theatrical entertainment or just solitude and the lonely sea and the sky — all were available on demand; no packing or formalities required, just offer your penny at the onion-domed kiosk and revolve with the turnstile. Should a harder-headed motive be summoned, then perhaps it is provided by the many thousands of steamboat passengers who tramped the motionless decks. Herne Bay pier was all of this.

Construction of a pier at Herne Bay was prompted by the proposed arrival of the General Steam Navigation Company's boats from London.

An Act was sought and obtained on 30th March, 1831. Besides authorising the construction of a pier, it incorporated the individual promoters as "The Herne Bay Pier Company." An elaborate table of tolls was scheduled to the Act — 10s. having to be paid for every billiard table conveyed, while bedsteads, mahogany, were rated at 9d. each and bedsteads, every other, at 6d. Public morality was also safe-guarded: section XCVII of the Act provided that any person who shall "from and after Six of the Clock in the Morning, and during so long as Day-light shall continue, undress himself on the Shore within One Mile of the said Pier or Jetty, or shall expose his naked Body to public View for the Purpose of bathing within the Distance aforesaid" would be liable to a fine or imprisonment!

Surveys were made by Thomas Rhodes, and his drawings, executed under the direction of the aged Thomas Telford and dated 27th November, 1830, may be seen today in Herne Bay Library. In essence, a T-shaped pier is shown with a double track tramway down its entire length (a feature not referred to in the legislation). The only connection between the tracks is a scissors crossover at the head of the pier. Before the seaward end, ramps branch off from either side of the pier and lead to a lower second level of the landing stage and, on these also, rails are shown.

---

123. Upper—Ramsgate East Cliff vertical lift in the early days.
Cliff Lifts Ltd.

124. Lower—The first Herne Bay Pier tram, from a water colour dated 10th February 1835, showing the tram taking steam boat passengers to the shore.
Block courtesy "Modern Tramway". Herne Bay Records Society.

If the finished pier and tramway were not as grand as the library watercolours would suggest, they were still remarkable. The deck was supported on timber piles shod with iron, five in a row, twenty feet between rows, sunk down to a bed of clay; whilst only twenty-four feet wide instead of the proposed thirty, the whole edifice extended for three thousand feet. The tramway was of single track, and was sail-powered.

Sir Henry Oxenden, a local land-owner and future subscriber to the pier, was studying at Cambridge in 1776 when he devised an ice yacht. This comprised a wooden frame with a skate at each corner. A table-cloth acted as sail and a pivoted Dragoon sword as rudder. After attaining an average speed of 24 miles per hour over a measured mile, further development resulted in a land yacht or "Sailing Machine." This 25 foot-long vehicle had front wheels 11 feet apart and steerable rear wheels three feet apart. The sails were described as "cutter rigged" and, with a crew of three, speeds of up to 30 miles per hour were made on Barham Downs. Perhaps due to Sir Henry's financial connection with the pier, his system was chosen to propel the "spacious and splendid conveyance, to be designated **Old Neptune's Car,** which will be used for the first time on the day of Mr. Hemsley's dinner," on 13th June, 1833. Failing sufficient wind, the car would be propelled by manual labour.

Literary fame was reached when the 'New Sporting Magazine' for October, 1834, told of the steamboat arrival of Mr. John Jorrocks, the cockney sportsman. *"What's this thing?" said he, to a ticket-porter, pointing to a sort of French diligence-looking concern which had just been pushed up to the landing end. "To carry the lumber, sir—live and dead—gentlemen and their bags, as don't like to walk." "Do you charge anything for the ride?" inquired J., with his customary caution. "Nothing" was the answer. "Then let's get on the roof" said J., "and take it easy, and survey the place as we go along." Accordingly we clambered on to the top of the diligence,* summa diligentia, *and seated ourselves on a pile of luggage as though we were on a triumphal car. The luggage being all stowed away, and as many passengers as it would hold put inside, two or three porters proceeded to propel the machine along the rail-road on which it runs.*

Having described the line, we act on the premise that there is nothing so intriguing as other peoples' misfortunes, and now progress to accidents. The Pier Master's Daily Record of Matters that Transpire upon Herne Bay Pier still exists, and on Tuesday, 2nd June, 1840 . . . 4.30 *arrived the Red Rover from London and saleed (sic) for Margate at 4.50, in coming up the Pier from the Rover I had the misfortune to run over a Poor Woman with a wooden Leg and went to Canterbury immediately with her to the Hospital.* The 'Kent Herald' for the 4th June ". . . Israel Jonas on suspicion of felony.

Discharged, the prosecution not appearing." The prosecutrix, Jane Harris, had died "from injuries, having been run over by Neptune Car." Did she fall, or was she pushed?

Captain Charles Cornelius Gardiner, the newly-appointed Pier Master, wrote to the Secretary of the Pier Company on 10th July, 1844. *I am sorry to Inform you of the Accident that took place on Wednesday evening a little before seven o'clock the Queen of the Thames Excursion Boat returning from Margate and calling at Herne Bay for a small party which they left behind in the morning we were proceeding down the Pier with the car and Lug Sail set with a moderate breeze from the Westward going at the rate of about 15 Miles per Hour when nearly at the End of the pier (George Norris) Jumped off to remove the tongues of the rail. Unfortunately the car ran over his right arm and was so much injured as obliged to take him to Canterbury Hospital and there Immediate Amputation took place. At present he is doing well. I should much like to know if I am to continue his wages. I shall do so until you advise me to the contrary.* We can guess that "the tongues of the rail" refers to a point; as to the fate of Norris, the Herne Bay Improvement Commissioners resolved on 2nd September "that the rate payable in respect of the occupation of a House by George Norris be abated in Consequence of his late serious loss of an arm."

As in all lives, as well as the tragic there is the comic, in this case provided by 'Punch.' The editor, Douglas Jerrold was a frequent visitor and in 1842 he satirised his arrival thus: *This landing place is strongly defended by two ships guns and six wheelbarrows. The garrison at present consists of four ticket porters, who are exercised two or three times a day, under the command of a glazed cap and a gold-laced band, in propelling a machine very like a diligence in reduced circumstances in which the steam boat passengers and luggage are conveyed at the rate of two pence per head and two pence per trunk.* Good humoured quips about Herne Bay were frequent in 'Punch' until an incident occurred about 1850 when the mood became scathing. Tradition holds that Jerrold was taking revenge. He had come to Herne Bay with his wife and she brought her new Parisien bonnet in a bonnet box. In landing, some clumsy porters contrived to crush this precious freight. Its mangled remains were conveyed on the tram car to the entrance gates when porterage was demanded . . . . This Mr. Punch, who was evidently much annoyed, at first indignantly refused. Finding protestation useless, however, the infuriated gentleman warned them that for the imposition he would make Herne Bay smart with ridicule — and Mr. Punch kept his word.

According to surviving correspondence, springs may have been fitted to one of the open cars in 1845. Little further is known about these pre-evolutionary trams. October, 1862, saw the last steamer at the pier

and an Act of 1865 empowered the Pier Company to take down and abandon a portion of the northern or seaward end of the pier. It is arguable that closure would have been forced anyway by the rapidly advancing decay wrought by the teredo worms. The pier was sold for scrap in 1871, but sometime before this date a remarkable event had occurred; the pier, complete with tram, was photographed. Having survived for over a hundred years, this distinctly indifferent print must be classed as one of the important landmarks in the photographic coverage of rail traction.

The Conduit Tram that took to Sea

HERNE BAY was destined to remain without a pier until 1873.
Two years' previously, the Herne Bay Promenade Pier Company, Limited obtained the Herne Bay Promenade Pier Order, which authorised that company to erect a new structure 80 yards east of the previous pier and some 1,100 yards in length. This pier was opened in 1873 by the Lord Mayor of London and was built of wood and iron. A shore-end pavilion was added in 1883.

The Order authorised the provision of tramways on the pier and the right to lease them for a term not exceeding seven years. The rates for using the tramway were not to exceed 3d. per passenger, 1d. per cubic foot for light goods and 2s. per ton for heavy goods. Tolls leviable on other pier users included 2d. "for every Bath or sedan chair," while "every perambulator including driver" would be charged 4d.

A further Order, secured in 1891, indicates that the company had by then changed its name to the Herne Bay Pier Company Limited. This Order permitted a further extension seawards of 1,200 yards and authorised the use of the tramway for the conveyance of passengers, animals, goods and merchandise by means of electricity, steam, mechanical or other motive power. The reference to electric traction at so early a date is particularly noteworthy.

The time for completing the new pier works was extended by the Herne Bay Pier Order 1896, which also imposed greater control on any tramway operation. Thus section 5 provided that any line constructed under the 1891 Order could not be used for the conveyance of passengers until it had been inspected and certified by the Board of Trade. Section 6 stated that unless with any electric operation of

---

125. Upper—The first Herne Bay Pier, built in 1832 and demolished in 1871, as it appeared in the 1860's complete with sail-powered tram & mast.　　　　　　　　　　　　　　Herne Bay Records Society.
126. Centre—The new Herne Bay Pier of 1898 under construction, showing conduit slot.　　　　　　　　　　　Herne Bay Records Society.
127. Lower—The new Herne Bay Pier electric tram as delivered.
　　　　　Block courtesy "Modern Tramway". "Lightning".

the tramway the power was "entirely contained in and carried along with the carriages" certain safeguards had to be employed: these were the fairly standard ones relating to insulated or low resistance returns, stray currents and electrolytic action. The Board of Trade was empowered to prescribe regulations in respect of the tramcars themselves.

A prospectus issued by the Pier Company in February, 1898, indicated that the extended pier would incorporate a tramway, which it was estimated should yield 85,000 twopenny fares, or about £700.

Photographs of the extension being constructed in 1898 show a crane running on a centrally-positioned track, the rails of which are laid flush with the deck. Later views of the nearly completed pier include a dramatic change; the crane and rails are still there but an off-centre conduit slot has appeared. Technical journals of the day insisted on describing the line as third rail and, as illustrations are scarce, this perhaps accounts for what up to now has been a virtually unknown application of conduit traction. The tramway was constructed by the British Thomson-Houston Company but, whilst they took out many patents about this time, no trace can be found on a shallow conduit suitable for the limited clearances, not more than six or nine inches, encountered in pier work. The conductor was 2 x 2 inch steel angle attached to porcelain insulators; other than this, no further details of the conduit are known. However, with the popularity of the pier for fishermen, trouble may have been experienced with bait and lines going down the slot; sea and salt air no doubt made their contribution, and what an opportunity for little boys with spades!

The running rails rested on 14-inch timbers run over the main girders and have been described both as 60-lb bullhead and 20-lb Vignoles, laid to a gauge of three feet. Comment on this dimension appears at the end of this section. The running rails were bonded at joints and crossbonded at 120-foot intervals. The conductor was joined by fishplates and double crown bonds. A cable led to the engine house situated in the shore-end pavilion. Power was generated by one of Messrs. J. E. H. Andrew's "Stockport" gas engines, specially built with two eight-foot flywheels for dynamo driving. The ball governor worked on the "hit and miss" principle; when the speed exceeded normal, it cut off the gas and allowed the engine an idle revolution. The usual anti-fluctuation gas bag and four circulation tanks were provided. Exhaust was passed through a silencer and ejected horizontally seawards.

A 13-inch belt connected one of the engine flywheels to a GE 50-kW multipole dc generator running at 600 revolutions per minute, and supplying current at 250 volts.

In passing, the carefully considered graduations of electric lighting may be noted. The pier buildings enjoyed about 246 "Robertson" incandescent lamps, whilst the pier proper had 24 "B.T.W." 110-hour enclosed arc lamps fixed at alternate sides of the pier. Round the pavilion were ten similarly arranged "Byng-Arnold" arc lamps and in front of the pier two "Solar" arc lamps stood on handsome standards. There were also two open-type "Blatwick" arc lamps.

Herne Bay received a welcome Christmas present in 1898 when two Peckham reversed maximum-traction trucks were delivered from the U.S.A. The car body arrived soon afterwards, and enabled a trial trip to be made in the third week of January, 1899. Major Cardew inspected the tramway on behalf of the Board of Trade on Friday, 17th March, 1899, public service commencing about Saturday, 1st April, at one penny per ride.

The Brush-built car was particularly handsome and, unlike most pier trams, would not have looked out of place in the street. It was powered by two General Electric 50-hp motors, taking an average current of 18 amp, and weighed nearly 7 tons. The official capacity was for 28 passengers though this was often exceeded. The installation was under the management of W. C. Dufton, the Pier Company's engineer.

The route was unusual, being flat, straight and with neither points nor depot; it ran between music and food. About 100 yards from the shore-end, the pier widened out for an as yet unbuilt pavilion. Dubbing for it was a marquee where the Cremona Orchestra and the Jollity Boys played or the band of the Tenth Hussars discoursed martial music. If you tired of sitting under your umbrella (for the marquee leaked), the tram would take you to the elegant octagonal restaurant at the pier head where "most recherché little dinners are daily served." As a protection against mishap a pair of buffers were installed by the restaurant door.

The tramway receipts for 1900 amounted to £424, which was £64 down on the previous year. In May, 1901, the line underwent a change; two regauged crossbench ex-horse cars arrived from Bristol. Built by the Bristol Carriage and Wagon Company for Bristol tramways, and each weighing about 32 cwt, they had become surplus as a result of the electrification of the Bristol system. One new car was placed at each end of the bogie car, and the latter's controllers were repositioned to the outer ends of the resulting train. Electric leads, links and pins, and permanently-attached chains coupled the now non-driving motor car to its two control trailers, No. 2 at the shore end and No. 3 at the restaurant end. At an unknown date, Dick, Kerr and Co. had supplied a luggage trolley which was pushed up the pier to the steamers, and here lay trouble.

On Tuesday, 16th July, 1901, the steam yacht *Cynthia* tied up on her way to Margate. As usual, the tram train started out to meet her, pushing the luggage trolley and keeping within its top speed of 5 miles per hour. Before starting, one of the directors, F. W. Wacher, decided

not to travel and got off the enclosed car, No. 1. The driver, George Harrison *(who had some four years experience on the tramway and in whom implicit confidence could be placed)* ejected the Managing Director's son from the front platform of the train, sending him to the rear car. Riding on the middle car, No. 1, to help with the brakes, was William Austin, a conductor of six weeks' experience. Generally there was an official on each car, but on this occasion the brakes of No. 2, the rear car, semed to have been unattended. Sarah and Thomas Pearce, both in their seventies and on holiday from Brixton, were seated in the first car with the driver. Suddenly, before the first 300 yards of the journey were covered, Thomas Pearce called out to Sarah, "hold tight they have rocked a truck." As he did so the luggage trolley, which was running light, left the track and veering to the left jammed itself between the railings and the first car. George Harrison *(in whom implicit confidence could be placed . . .)* seeing the serious and dangerous position jumped off the car. The conductor and two passengers also jumped. Unfortunately the speed with which the staff reacted did not leave them any time to apply the brakes. The first car with several passengers crashed through the railings to the right and somersaulted down into the water. Thomas Pearce supported his wife in the water until she was picked up by a rowing boat and, even though he knew that she was dead, refused to be taken in, but went to another lady's assistance. In the meantime the conductor recovered his sense of responsibility sufficently to throw lifebelts into the sea from the pier. Many boats floated over the car and attempts were made to change its position by coastguards and divers, as it was feared that there might be more bodies underneath.

The pier was closed within a half hour and the scheduled appearance of the Jollity Boys abandoned, but this did not perturb the holidaymakers. They had a far more interesting spectacle as they crowded the promenade watching the doctor working on the beach and waiting expectantly for low tide and the thrill of additional bodies being discovered. Happily they waited in vain.

Over 50 feet of pier railings had been damaged and the leading bogie of the motor car was off the track. The two remaining cars were pushed back to the beginning of the pier and preparations made for the inquest, which was held at 6.30 p.m. At the inquest the coroner was told that Mrs. Pearce's skull had separated from her scalp

---

128. Upper—After the accident on 16th July 1901, Car No. 1 and control-trailer on the pier and No. 3 in the water.
Herne Bay Records Society.
129. Centre—Still apparently sound, No. 3 is moored against the rising tide while boatmen bring out sightseers.   Herne Bay Records Society.
130. Lower—No. 3 back in service without the infamous luggage trailer and a fender to sweep aside obstructions.
Blocks courtesy "Modern Tramway".   Courtesy A. A. Jackson.

by six inches, that the conductor thought the bogie car to be a six-wheeler and that the driver was only a driver and did not exactly know how the motive power was communicated to the cars. When pressed by a juror, the coroner said that he did not intend to inform the Board of Trade of the accident, and further that he considered no blame for the accident to attach to anybody. The only note of sanity came from the jury, who, by way of an expression of opinion, stated that pushing the trolley should be discontinued. After the inquest No. 3 was floated ashore in the early hours of the morning looking, very little shaken for its eventful wanderings.

Due to the feelings of a Mr. Green, the Board of Trade were not cheated out of their inquiry, Major Pringle, R.E., arriving in Herne Bay on the following Tuesday. The inquiry was private and, although publication of its findings was promised, they do not seem to have been reported. Said the 'Herne Bay Press', *"Who is Green" has been asked, and why should he have been so interested as to wire the Board of Trade? He is, however, believed to be well-known, and rumour attaches, we know not how truly, a motive not altogether friendly, and probably activated by feelings that will bring him no credit.*

The Press insisted on treating the accident in the same sensational manner as if it had been a full-size train smash, even breathlessly reporting the names of those people who missed the tram or were detained by business from travelling on it. Uproar broke out at Woolwich Arsenal when the 'Evening News,' mistaking the crash for an accident to that day's excursion train to Herne Bay from Bexley Heath, reported death and destruction in full measure. So effective was the power of the press that a number of men ran home in terror to see what had happened to their wives and children.

The accounts for 1901 and 1902 show that compensation of nearly £300 was paid, and also that tram fares for the two years were down to £282 and £260 respectively. On the pier as a whole losses were mounting, and these were aggravated by the substantial amounts of debenture interest due. In 1905, H. C. Jones, the General Manager and owner of the local 'Argus' newspaper went bankrupt. The 'Argus' closed, and Jones went to prison for five years for embezzlement. The pier soon fell into the hands of debenture holders and on 17th February, 1905, a receiver was appointed. It was then discovered that the existing Pier Orders gave him no power to sell the undertaking and it was accordingly necessary to obtain the Herne Bay Pier Act 1908 to achieve this. The pier was then sold on 5th November, 1908,

131. Upper—The petrol-electric tram of 1925 complete with crew.
C. J. Henley.
132. Centre—The petrol-electric tram in service (Right) the same derelict in front of the car shed, February 1948 (Left). J. H. Meredith.
133. Lower—The new battery-Electric tram of 1934 running solo.
Blocks courtesy "Modern Tramway". Electric Power Storage Co.

to the Herne Bay Urban District Council. What had cost about £60,000 was bought by the Council for £6,000. The transaction was completed in September, 1909, an event which was marked by running up the U.D.C. flag on the pavilion.

Shortly before the transfer the pier had been damaged by a barge running into it during a gale, and this had necessitated the tram stopping short of the restaurant. The town replaced the marquee with a proper pavilion, but otherwise nothing of note happened until the outbreak of the war in 1914, when the steamers ceased to call. With them, the reason for the tram also departed.

After the war the generator was taken over by the local electricity supplier and the pier connected to the town mains. The trams are reputed to have been used as shelters on the pier prior to being sold to a Rochester firm for scrap.

The Tramway that was blown up

THE resumption of peace saw the return of the steamboats and with them demand for a pier tram. This was at a time when, in addition to large well-known car builders, small firms, each capable of producing only a handful of cars a year, existed. The Strode Engineering Company, producer of the 'Westcar,' had its shed in Herne Bay. By reasoning now unknown, the Pier and Entertainments Committee decided that a locally-built petrol-electric tram would be ideal for the pier. In February, 1925, plans were submitted to the Ministry of Transport for approval. The tram was to cost £814 and the track was to be modified for an additional £200 in accordance with the previous instructions of the Ministry. Probably it was at this stage that the conduit was removed. The steamboat company agreed to pay 1d. for every passenger landed, to be increased to 2d. when the wings of the pier were ready.

Formal sanction for raising a loan having been granted, the tram was delivered in July, 1925, and first used on August Bank Holiday. Delivery was complicated by the presence of the pavilion now on the site of the old marquee. Whilst heralding the rebirth of the tramway, the new car was also the last vehicle to be built by Strode. Mr. Wilding, who used to drive the tram and still works on the pier, recalls that the petrol engine was in the centre of the car and projected two thirds above the floor. There was a petrol tank at the shore end, and the roof carried a water tank which often boiled. The dynamo was connected to the petrol engine by a chain which, like the water, frequently caused trouble.

In 1934 it was estimated that the tram had lost £60 in fares through having been out of service for 11½ days during the previous year. Also, there had been a very great increase of passengers landed in steam boats (sic), so a new tram was clearly required. As a result the

Surveyor drew up an estimate of the initial outlay and running costs for battery, diesel-electric and, here it is hard not to express surprise at what may have been the last serious proposal of its type, cable traction. Out of this, two schemes ensued, both for battery cars. Scheme I was for a new 48-seat car with two controllers and an 11-hp Metrovick motor, and the existing petrol electric tram to be fitted with electrical conrol and Lockheed hydraulic braking, so arranged that it could be run as a control trailer with the new battery tram as required. Scheme 2 called for a new battery car as well as rebuilding the existing car into a battery car, the two cars to be run singly or together. As there was neither a passing loop nor the room for one this scheme was rather pointless, so it is not surprising that the tender of F. C. Hibberd and Co. Ltd. of London for £1,049 10s. 0d. for the first scheme was accepted. Ministry of Transport sanction for a loan was received in April, 1934 and in August a substantial payment was made to Hibberd. The date on which the new tram arrived is not clear, but it is reasonable to assume that it was about this time.

A month later when the *Queen of Kent* tied up, a seaman fell overboard and was struck by a paddle wheel. Fortunately he survived and was taken by tram to the ambulance. At some stage, perhaps in the petrol-electric period, a corrugated iron shed large enough for one car was erected at the shore end of the line. The old conduit-tram buffers were left in place at each end of the track, but one resident at the time, Mr. R. S. Bamford, says that "the inner set was behind the tram shed wall, because I seem to recall thinking that if a car ran over and hit the buffers, it would have to demolish the shed wall first!" The tram was charged in the shed, the batteries having been supplied by the D.P. Battery Co. In 1937 the battery capacity was increased by about 40 per cent with the introduction of the Kathanode cell, type K27. The K27 cell, of which 33 were required to make the complete battery, had a capacity of 364 ampere-hours with a 5 hour rate of discharge. Each cell measured 6.3 x 8.8 inches and was 13.9 inches high. The overall weight of the battery was about 2,600lb.

Timetable running, with the first and last cars at 10.45 a.m. and 9.30 p.m. respectively, was introduced in 1936. Difficulties experienced in boarding and alighting from the narrow running boards required low platforms to be constructed at each end of the line. In 1938, the awnings on the tram and trailer were damaged during a storm and the replacements cost £50. Notice boards, erected in 1939, announced a 15-minute service from 9.30 a.m. to 6.00 p.m.

Then came the war. As part of the defence precautions the pier was taken over by the military, barbed wire unrolled, and sandbags piled high. On 3rd November, 1939, Mr. Wilding drove the tram to the shore end, and soon afterwards two sections of the pier were blown

134. Two car train at Hereson Road Station, with the yellow control trailer leading.　　　Block courtesy "Modern Tramway". Photo J. H. Price.

up to prevent its use by an invading force. The trams remained until after the war before being sold for £12 10s. 0d., though the more valuable brass and copper parts went earlier to the scrap drive.

Today, as the future of the now aged pier is again under discussion, the arrow-straight track, severed just before each end as a result of the war measures, and further isolated following a fire in 1970, remains to tease us with a mystery. Measure the gauge yourself — you will find it is 3 feet 4.5 inches, but don't ask why. Like the Sphinx, it keeps the secret of its riddle.

THE RAMSGATE TUNNEL RAILWAY

Whilst the Isle of Thanet tramways were in their last months of operation, electric passenger transport came to the area in a new form. Running beneath Ramsgate from the Harbour to Dumpton Park is the Dumpton Tunnel, a railway tunnel opened in 1863 by the London, Chatham & Dover Railway to give access to their terminus at Ramsgate Harbour. The tunnel was difficult to operate with steam traction, with a 1 in 75 gradient from a standing start, and in July, 1926 the Southern Railway closed this section of line and diverted the railway to a new Ramsgate Station at the back of the town.

Ramsgate Harbour Station was taken over by the Corporation and leased to Thanet Amusements Ltd. who ran it as the Pleasureland Amusement Park. They decided to make use of the derelict tunnel and instal a narrow gauge railway worked by electricity, with the double object of bringing people from the Dumpton Park area to their amusement park and offering a tunnel ride with illuminated tableaux as an attraction. It was christened the World Scenic Railway and had artificial scenery depicting each of the larger countries of the world, such as the Pyramids of Egypt, the giant redwood trees of California and the temples of India. There was ample room, as the old tunnel was built to take a double track of standard gauge.

276

The lower station was placed at the southern exit of Dumpton Tunnel, in the amusement park, but to provide a suitable outlet and terminus at Dumpton a branch tunnel was built, 8 ft. by 6 ft., with a gradient of 1 in 15, emerging in a cutting and ending with a two-track terminal station at Hereson Road. The gauge chosen was two feet, with 30lb./yd. flat bottom rail on wooden sleepers, and contracts were placed through the Holborn Construction Company with English Electric early in 1936 for all mechanical and constructional work. They were given the 'go ahead' to start work in May, and it was stipulated that the line must open by the August Bank Holiday. A penalty would be payable if it was not completed on time, and a bonus if it was! Thus every effort was put into getting the line and rolling stock completed, with staff from Preston working long hours of overtime, sustained by free beer. For the same reason, standard mining equipment was chosen for the motive power, rather than spend time on designing something new.

These efforts were crowned with success, and the railway was opened on 31st July, 1936, by Mr. E. C. Cox, Traffic Manager of the Southern Railway. The line was three-quarters of a mile long, and of single track with a passing loop at the half-way point and with two platform tracks at each terminus. 780 yards was inside the former railway tunnel, and the remainder was new construction. There was no depot, the stock being kept on a siding just inside the lower end of the tunnel, where there was also a substation. A floodlit effect of the artificial scenery was obtained by lamps fixed to the trains, which lit up the scenery in passing. Current was obtained from the Isle of Thanet company at 400 volts a.c. and converted by a motor-generator set to the line voltage of 460 d.c. The line ran only in the summer months.

In September, 1939 the railway closed, and the tunnel became part of Ramsgate's deep shelter system against air raids. New small-diameter tunnels were driven from the side of the main tunnel to connect with various street entrances. The railway reopened at Whitsuntide, 1946, the proprietors now being Ramsgate Olympia Ltd., who changed the name of the amusement park to Merrie England. The original motor-generator set was replaced by a small mercury-arc rectifier. The prewar scenery was replaced by illuminated tableaux, which were switched on and off by the passage of the trains through contact skates on the grooved trolley wire. Some of the tableaux were purchased second-hand in various years from Blackpool Illuminations.

The railway ran without incident from 1946 to 1956. The original running time was $4\frac{1}{2}$ minutes, but trains frequently took rather longer so as to allow passengers a good view of the tableaux. No timetable was issued; the driver of one or other train signalled with a hand-generator and bell the fact that he had some passengers, whereupon

135. Ramsgate Tunnel Railway. The lower terminus at "Olympia," after the cliff fall in 1957 had necessitated the replacement of the former tunnel mouth by a concrete wall. Locomotive end of yellow train.

Photo: J. H. Price.
Block courtesy "Modern Tramway".

the other driver acknowledged the signal and both trains would start, meeting at the half-way loop. This loop was provided with illuminated spring points and protected by colour-light signals showing green or amber. The signal equipment was by Westinghouse and was based on 8 volt a.c. track circuiting with tripcocks. Only when the single line ahead was unoccupied and the spring points re-set would the signal clear to green; if a train were to proceed against the amber signal, it would be stopped by the tripcock actuating the train's Westinghouse air brake. The fares in the early 1950s were 3d single and 6d return (adult and child) with Williamson tickets torn from a roll.

On 15th February, 1957, part of the tunnel collapsed at the lower end, and was replaced by a new concrete retaining wall, with a small single track entrance; both termini became single tracked, and the rolling stock siding in the lower part of the tunnel was extended to form a loop. The railway remained closed throughout 1957, but re-opened in the summer of 1958.

On 1st July, 1965, a descending train became out of control in the tunnel, ran away, failed to stop at Olympia terminus, and crashed through the buffers into the wall of a building. The leading car was damaged beyond repair, the driver being seriously injured. The other train maintained a twenty minute service until the end of the season, running for the last time on 26th September, 1965, after which the railway closed. In 1966 it was decided not to reopen, and the plant was sold off. Most of the 50 lb. rails (which had replaced the original 30 lb. rails in 1947-8) went to the Romney, Hythe & Dymchurch Light Railway, and the seven surviving passenger coaches were sold to Lieut.-Commander J. M. Baldock of Liphook, Hants, who has used two of them since 1971, on a steam operated pleasure line, the Hollycombe Woodland Railway. Three more are in store there, and the other two were taken over in 1970 by the Hampshire Narrow Gauge Railway Society for use on a short 2 ft. gauge private railway at Durley, Hampshire; one is now in use. The tunnel at Ramsgate is now boarded up.

However, narrow gauge electric traction lived on until very recently in East Kent in the form of an extensive 550 volt underground railway system at Chislet Colliery, installed in 1963 to replace battery traction. English Electric was again the supplier.

Rolling Stock

Two four car trains were built for the Ramsgate Tunnel Railway by English Electric in 1936. They were unnumbered but were distinguished by colour, one train being painted red and the other yellow.

At the outer ends of each four-car train was a small four-wheel electric locomotive of a type used for haulage in mines, and ballasted to weigh seven tons. On this unit rested the forward end of the first car, so forming an articulated unit. The driver rode in the end of the coach, which was fitted with jumper cables, air brake controls, and an English Electric type 10A controller with dead-man's handle. The inner end of these coaches rode on a bogie and between them were coupled two bogie trailers, all trailing axles having roller-bearing axleboxes. Seating was of cross-bench layout, with three passengers abreast, and the complete red train seated 108 persons (motor-cars 24 and trailers 30). In the yellow train there were intermediate controls, allowing two half-trains to be run, and the red train was altered similarly after the war, reducing its capacity to 102. Current was taken by short trolley poles, mounted on bases, with swivelling sliding contact collector shoes. All stock was fitted with Westinghouse Air brakes and twin lighting circuits (mains and battery), and powerful electric headlamps were carried on the locomotives and control trailers. The coach bodies were built in teak on welded steel underframes.

The lower-end motor coach of the yellow train was damaged beyond repair in the 1965 runaway and was broken up, after which the red train maintained the service until closure. The two control trailers from the yellow train are now at Durley, the intermediate cars of the red train are in use at Hollycombe, and the three surviving motor coaches (with one bogie each) are stored at the Hollycombe farm.

MARGATE JETTY.

We conclude this chapter with a brief mention of Margate Jetty which lies opposite the Metropole Hotel. A scheme to build a jetty,

139. Locomotive "Caledonia" with Ramsgate Tunnel Railway Coaches on
Hollycombe Woodland Garden Railway.
Block courtesy "Modern Tramway".   J. H. Price.

tramway and sea wall was proposed in 1868 by the Margate Pier &
Tramway Co., who intended to buy out the Margate Harbour Company. The share capital was to be £120,000 and the tramway on the
Jetty was to be 26 chains in length and of 4 ft. 8½ in. gauge. A similar
scheme was put up in 1869 by another company and they presented
Bills in 1869 and 1870 respectively. The outcome was that the better
points of the 1870 Bill were taken over by the former company, but
this was wound up on 24th July 1893.

Evidently another Bill was deposited with a plan in 1899, as the
Margate Pier and Harbour Act of 1900, permitted the construction of
a single 3 ft. 6 in. gauge tramway line for the length of the jetty and
the owners were permitted to charge 2 pence per person for travelling
on the tramway.

The line was evidently constructed and used, but little else is known,
save that the rails, apparently of standard gauge and long since disused, were in position until 1945. There is now a miniature railway
on the jetty, under the same ownership as that in the Dreamland
Amusement Park.

Opposite.
136. Upper—Locomotive No. 1 "Billie" of the Dreamland Railway.
Photo J. H. Meredith.
137. Centre—Short train at Hereson Road station of Ramsgate Tunnel
Railway in 1953.   Photo J. H. Meredith.
138. Lower—Ex-Ramsgate Tunnel coaches at the sandpit terminus of
Hollycombe Woodland Railway in 1972.
Photo J. H. Price.

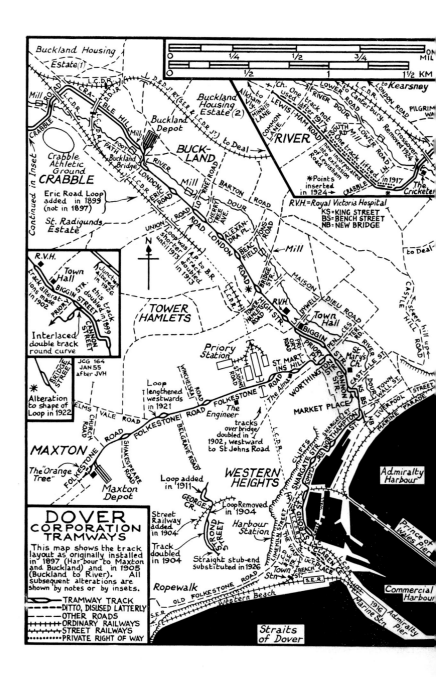

CHAPTER SEVEN

DOVER CORPORATION TRAMWAYS

History and Topography

THE Channel port of Dover, gateway to England for a large proportion of foreign visitors, dates from Roman times. It is built on the banks and silted-up estuary of the River Dour, a small chalk stream which flows for the last two miles of its course through a valley about half a mile wide, between hills 250 to 300 feet high, running roughly northwest and southeast. The high ground on the east is almost unbroken, but on the west side there are two dry valleys and a short combe.

At the south end the main valley gives upon the foreshore, which is in the form of a crescent about a mile long, with a promenade giving an unbroken view of the Admiralty Harbour and the shipping within its three sheltering walls, the Eastern Arm, the detached Southern Breakwater and the Western Arm or Admiralty Pier. The River Dour, which once had two mouths, now flows into the sea westwards through a brick conduit opening into Wellington Basin, the innermost of the Western Docks, which though not exactly on the same site, have nevertheless developed directly from the primative port of Tudor times in the extreme south-west corner of the bay, long ago silted up and built over.

The former South Eastern Railway reached Dover via Folkestone on 7th February 1844, approaching along the foreshore to a terminal called "Dover Town", with an extension to the Admiralty Pier, where later it met the L.C. & D.R.

The London, Chatham and Dover Railway reached Dover on 22nd July 1861 and entered the town at the head of the valley on the east side, crossing the Dour on a high embankment and then running in a cutting and tunnel on the west side with a station, Dover Priory, on

139. Opposite—Map of the Dover Corporation Tramways system.
J. C. Gillham.

140. Above—The badge carried on Dover Corporation trams, not a true coat of arms but a pleasing design made up from the official seals of the town.
Drawn by G. E. Baddeley.

the Folkestone Road, near the foot of the longest side valley and close to the centre of the town. The line continues in another tunnel, beneath the lofty ridge of the Western Heights to a point close to the "Tidal Basin", or "Outer Harbour" where there was formerly a terminal station "Dover Harbour" with an extension onto the Admiralty Pier, on which in 1916, the Marine Station was built to replace the former shelterless passenger facilities at the Cross-Channel packet berths. Neither the "Harbour Station" nor the former S.E.R. "Dover Town" station now exist. There is also a line to Deal, which branches off the L.C. & D.R. line at Buckland and crosses the valley on a high embankment and a connecting line across the "Pier District".

By the end of the 19th Century the town had grown more than a mile up the main valley from the shore and had spread into the western side valleys and part of the way up the eastern hillside, below and northwards from Dover Castle, but the only public transport provided was by privately owned horse buses. However on 9th November 1895, the Council passed a resolution proposing the construction of an electric tramway system in the borough. Application was made to Parliament and authority was obtained under the Tramways Order Confirmation (No. 1) Act of 1896, to construct the following lines:—

Tramway No. 1. Length — 8.3 chains, of which 6.8 chains were to be single line and 1.5 chains double line.
Commencing at the junction of Beach Street with Clarence Place and Passing along Clarence Place and Crosswall, terminating at a point 1.7 Chains south of the junction of Crosswall with Strond Street.

Tramway No. 2. Length — 2 miles 2 furlongs 5.4 chains, of which 1 mile 7 furlongs 5.4 chains were to be single line and 3 furlongs to be double line.
Continuation of Tramway No. 1, in Crosswall and passing thence along Strond Street, the "George Inn" corner, Snargate Street, Court's Corner, Northampton Street, New Bridge, Bench Street, King Street, Market Place (later known as Market Square) Cannon Street, Biggin Street, High Street, London Road, and Canterbury Road, terminating on the southern side of the bridge carrying the road over the Kearsney to Deal branch of the London, Chatham and Dover Railway.

Tramways Nos. 3 & 4. These were short sections in the Pier district, put up as alternatives to Tramway No. 1, instead of Strond Street, but were not authorized.

Tramway No. 5. Length — 9.2 chains, of which 7.7 chains were to be single line and 1.5 chains double line.

Commencing in Northampton Street by a junction with Tramway No. 2 at a point 0.5 chains west of the junction of Northampton Street with New Bridge and passing thence along New Bridge and Camden Crescent and terminating at a point 0.5 chains east of the junction of Wellesley Place and Liverpool Street.

Tramway No. 6. An alternative to Tramway No. 5 in Townwall Street, not authorized.

Tramway No. 7. Length — 2 furlongs 8.3 chains whereof 2 furlongs 3.8 chains were to be single line and 4.5 chains to be double line.
A continuation of Tramway No. 5 in Liverpool Street and proceeding via Douro Place and East Cliff Road, terminating at the westerly junction of East Cliff Back Road.

Tramway No. 8. Length — 1 furlong 4.5 chains. All single line.
A continuation of Tramway No. 7 along East Cliff Road to the easterly junction of East Cliff Road and the road leading to East Cliff Back Road.

Tramway No. 9. An alternative to Tramway No. 8 in East Cliff Back Road — not authorized.

Tramway No. 10. Length 5 furlongs 7.3 chains, whereof 4 furlongs 5.3 chains were to be single line and 1 furlong 2 chains to be double line.
Commencing at a junction with Tramway No. 2 in Biggin Street opposite Pencester Road and passing thence along Worthington's Lane (later known as Worthington Street), Priory Place and Folkestone Road, to Elms Road (later known as Elms Vale Road).

Tramway No. 11. Length — 5 furlongs 4.28 chains, whereof 5 furlongs 1.28 chains were to be single line and 3.0 chains to be double line.
A continuation of Tramway No. 10 in Folkestone Road as far as the Borough Boundary.

Tramway No. 12. Length — 8.4 chains, whereof 6.9 chains were to be single line and 1.5 chains to be double line.
Commencing in Priory Place by a junction with Tramway No. 10 at a point 1.2 chains northwest of the junction of Priory Place with Military Road and passing thence in a northwesterly direction along Priory Place and Priory Road and terminating at a junction with Tramway No. 2 at the junction of Biggin Street and Effiingham Crescent.

Provided that this tramway shall not be constructed if so much of Tramway No. 2 as is by this Order authorized to be laid in Biggin Street between the junctions of that street with Worthington's Lane and Priory Road shall be constructed.

Construction of the Tramways

Stephen Sellon Assoc. M.I.C.E. was appointed Consulting Engineer and before completing his report, he made comparison between electric operation and the merits of the Lührig Gas System, which was being pressed by the Dover Gas Company. The contracts for the construction of the tramways were given to Messrs. Dick, Kerr & Co. Ltd. and were their first for electric tramway equipment.

700 tons of tram rail arrived by sea in S.S. "Pearl" at Dover on 11th March 1897, and construction work on the main line — Pier-Market Place-Buckland, i.e. Tramways Nos. 1 & 2 and the Folkestone Road branch line, Worthington's Lane-Folkestone Road, i.e. Tramways Nos. 10 & 11 commenced early in 1897. The track was laid to the 3 ft. 6 in. gauge, with single track and passing loops, as indicated on the route map. Girder rails 30 feet long and weighing 87 lb. to the yard were laid, using "Dicker" joints to connect them to each other. These joints were made with four-bolt fishplates flush with the top of the rail, which was cut out to accommodate them; this joint was supposed to present a continuous surface to the wheels, but in practice it did nothing of the sort and made three joints where there need only have been one, with consequent unnecessary noise. The track was laid on continuous blocks of Portland Concrete 12 x 8 inches, and kept to correct gauge by tie-bars. The space between the foundations was filled with 6 inches of floating concrete, over which was laid half an inch of sand and on this rested the paving setts of Guernsey granite.

The overhead wires were suspended at a height of 21 feet 6 inches above the road surface, attached to poles which were erected mainly on the south side of the road, by fixed insulators mounted on short bracket arms, except in King Street and the Market Square, where double bracket centre posts were used. Electric current was supplied by the Dover Electricity Company, from their power station in Park Street where additional equipment was installed to cope with the increased load.

Tramway No. 2 was built only as far as Buckland Bridge and Tramways Nos. 10 & 11, the Folkestone Road line, only as far as the foot of Maxton Hill, making a route mileage of 3 miles 6.15 chains in all. Tramway Nos. 7, 8 & 9 were not built.

Depots

Two depots were provided, one near the outer terminus of each line. At Buckland Bridge the single terminal track continued across the road into a four track depot, which was constructed to hold twenty

141. Line up of cars before the opening, showing No. 10 as a trailer. Photographed near Cherry Tree Avenue.   Cassiers' Magazine.

cars; inspection pits were provided in the centre two roads, but there were no other facilities for repairs, which had to be carried out in the two road, six car depot at Maxton, whose connecting spurs turned out of the running line just short of the terminal loop. For the opening of the system, ten double deck cars (two of which were trailers) were ordered through the Dick, Kerr organization and were built by Brush, with Peckham trucks from America. (See Rolling Stock section for full details.)

Work on the main line, except for the short section from Beach Street to Crosswall was completed in the summer of 1897.

Inspection and Opening

The main line was examined by the Board of Trade Inspector, Major Marindin, on 27th August and the official opening took place on 6th September 1897, when a car was driven by the Mayor, but there was no other ceremony; this made Dover the first electric tramway to open in the south of England, by quite a wide margin. The Folkestone Road line was inspected on 10th December and it was opened soon afterwards. However, difficulty was experienced with the Clarence Pier section (Tramway No. 1) because of a much used railway level crossing. Its completion and inspection dates are not known, but were probably late in January 1898. Even then working was not satisfactory and the line was abandoned in April, but the rails remained in place for some years afterwards.

The General Manager appointed at the opening was Mr. E. C. Carden, who held the post for 20 years.

The early abandonment of the short section of line in Clarence Place, beyond the level crossing at the Crosswall, resulted in a marked

287

142. Car No. 4 with "Providence" life guard, running from New Bridge into the single track in Bench Street.   Dover Corporation.

improvement of the service, as the trams were no longer delayed by the frequent closure of the gates at this busy railway crossing. It seems that after the acquisition of two more cars, Nos. 11 & 12, in the middle of 1898, a five minute service was provided on the main line and a ten minute service on Folkestone Road. Two further cars, Nos. 13 & 14 were delivered within the next few months. The following year saw the arrival of two more cars, this time from America. In the same year, 1899, the track was doubled from King Street as far as the "interlacing lines" in the upper part of Biggin Street and the Junction at Worthington Street was replaced by a layout with inter-lacing curves. On 5th April 1900, the Council approved the purchase of a track cleaning and water car, which was delivered in due course.

Also in 1900, signalling apparatus was installed in Strond Street, Snargate Street and Northampton Street to guard the blind curves at George Corner and Court's Corner; signals were also installed in Folkestone Road to cover the long stretch of single track from Priory Station to Winchlsea Road. The down track in Upper Biggin Street was removed and cars used the former up track in both directions, enabling other vehicles to stand in the 9 ft. 6 in. margin on the east side. An additional loop was constructed at Eric Road, dividing the very long single track section between Cherry Tree Avenue and Buckland Bridge.

The only item of interest in 1901, was a wedding by tram on 19th April and in 1902, the Corporation initiated the first moves to acquire the Dover Electricity Supply Co., which they achieved in 1904. The first moves were also made, although not by the Corporation, towards the construction of two extensions. Private syndicates applied for permission to construct a route over the authorized East Cliff line and continuing to St. Margaret's-at-Cliffe and Martin Mill. (See Chapter on "Proposed Tramways" for further details). The other proposal was for a line from Buckland Bridge, up Crabble Hill as authorized in 1896, but turning left a few yards short of the boundary, down a steep cut, subsequently known as Crabble Road and thence resuming a northerly direction over a private right of way to the village of River, a total distance of about 1¼ miles; a further portion extending about ¾ mile into the Alkham Valley was not authorized. The Order for the line was made on 12th October 1903.

The initial moves were also made for the improvement of the Pier district: the part with which we are chiefly concerned was the construction of an elevated road or viaduct, eliminating the troublesome railway crossing at Clarence Place. The tramway in Strond Street would have been abandoned and replaced by a new double track line along this route.

A more modern car No. 17 with reversed stairs was acquired in 1902. Meanwhile, the track was doubled in the upper end of Biggin Street, as far as the Royal Victoria Hospital, also for the full length of Priory Station Bridge and its approaches. These works were completed by March 1904, when the passing loop at the eastern end of Strond Street was removed to enable the railway company to construct a railway line on the street, which was to cross the tram line at "The George" corner, where special renewable castings had to be supplied to support the tram wheels across the wider railway flangeways. To compensate, the remaining passing loop in Strond Street was lengthened. The Atlantic Liner traffic for which the railway was built, lasted only until 1906, but the street railway remained in use for goods traffic. In April 1904, an experimental top cover was purchased from Messrs. Milnes & Voss for £75 and fitted to car No. 14. However, it had to be removed in 1905 when the Board of Trade forbade the use of top covers on narrow gauge seaside or hilly tramway systems. It was then used as an elevated foreman's office in Maxton Depot, reached by an old tram staircase.

The Extension to River

Acute unemployment in the later part of 1904 induced the Council to look round for relief schemes and with this in view, they took over

143. An early view of Maxton Depot with cars Nos. 11 & 5.

E. H. Bond.

the Powers of the River Light Railway Syndicate and commenced the construction of the line. This was laid as double track throughout, with a trailing crossover half way along, near the "Cricketers" Inn, at the foot of Crabble Road; from the North Gate of the Athletic Ground to South Road, River, the line was laid on private track on sleepers and ballasted; there were two level crossings, one for farm stock and the other for ordinary traffic. The terminus at River consisted of a single track stub and in order that intending passengers in Minnis Lane should be able to see a waiting car, it had to be driven to the very end of the rails. On Crabble Hill the rail joints were staggered, so that the cars gave out a four beat rhythm like a bogie car. The Light Railway Order included that part of Tramway No. 2 which had not been completed from its former terminus at Buckland Bridge and for which powers had now expired; this also was laid in double track.

The work was sufficiently complete for a trial trip to be made during September 1905, followed by the Board of Trade Inspection by Major Pringle on or about 29th September. The official opening took place

144. Upper—Car No. 10 with Providence lifeguard in the early days after
it had been motorized.   Courtesy Ray Warner.
145. Lower—Car No. 11 with a slightly later lifeguard at River terminus.
                                          Courtesy Tramway Museum Society.

on the 2nd October 1905, the first car being driven by the Right Hon.
George Wyndham, M.P. for Dover.

For this extension, four new cars were purchased for £575 each;
these were similar to No. 17, but had normal half turn staircases
instead of reversed, various other detail differences and slipper brakes
were also acquired for the existing cars, so that all could run to River,
but it was also found necessary to obtain eight shorter trolley masts
to replace those originally fitted to the first batch of cars and later

146. The opening of the River extension. Car No. 21 dressed with
bunting is in the foreground.   Courtesy W. J. Wyse.

changed around, but then still in use, possibly because they were too
tall to pass under the bridge in Crabble Road. ("Tramway & Railway
World" reports that this type of mast proved unsatisfactory — particularly at Leeds).

We now pass on to the year 1911, when Sunday tram services were
first introduced and another unsuccessful attempt was made to run a
through service between the Pier and Maxton. Possibly connected
with this was the construction of an additional passing loop, very short
and sharply curved at "The George" corner.

In 1912 some of the rails left abandoned in Clarence Place, were
taken up and used in the construction of a siding in New Bridge,*
to accommodate cars awaiting the end of band performances in
Granville Gardens and other entertainments on the sea fronts. Three
more new cars, Nos. 22-24 were also acquired in that year. They
were similar to Nos. 18-21, but were built by Brush. These cars always
ran well and were very quiet. There was a small illuminated transparency under the canopy, inscribed "River" and a metal flap which
could cover it when the car was not working on that section.

In 1913 the single track in the upper part of the High Street was
relaid and tenders for the construction of the viaduct across the Pier
district and for the new tramway thereon were invited, but the outbreak of war in the following year brought the scheme to a standstill.
Meanwhile, the track was doubled in the vicinity of a blank wall and
elevated carriageway, known as Buckland Terrace and the Cherry Tree
Avenue loop was lengthened; these with some other improvements
cost £1,500.

*"New Bridge" is the name of a short street leading from Bench Street
to the sea front.

The 1914-1918 War and Crabble Road Accident.

During the war, there was a serious shortage of spare parts and other materials also of manpower, consequently the state of the undertaking deteriorated considerably; the only recorded improvement was the installation of an automatic signal light operated by Folkestone Road cars as they approached Worthington Street, to ensure that connections were made with main line cars. Later, women conductors were taken on and even three women drivers were employed. In 1915, Mr. E. H. Bond, was appointed Electrical Works Superintendent.

On 19th August 1917 a very serious accident occurred to car No. 20, when bound for River. It got out of control at the top of Crabble Hill, ran away down the gradient of 1 in 10 in Crabble Road and overturned at the bottom, killing eleven passengers and injuring sixty. Consequently cars ceased running on this section.

Colonel Pringle R.E. of the Board of Trade held an Inquiry on 24th August and stated that the service over the River section could be resumed as soon as the car was removed and this was done on 30th August. At the Inquiry it was revealed that the driver, although shaken was unhurt, having jumped off before it reached the bottom. He stated that the hand brake was useless, the slipper brake would not hold the car and the emergency brake handle had jammed. When the car was examined shortly after the accident the hand brake chain was indeed found to be off the hook, but as there were no marks to indicate that it had been trailing on the ground, it seemed reasonable to conclude that it had become unshipped when the car overturned and not before; moreover, the driver admitted that the brake had worked at Buckland. The blocks of the slipper brake were acknowledged to be somewhat worn, but witnesses for the Corporation claimed that they were quite servicable. The controller was brought into court; the mechanism was explained and found to be faultless, but the witness stated that he had found the key in the forward position and the main handle at full parallel. It seems probable therefore, that the reason why the rheostatic brake would not work was that the driver had not switched off power, but had actually driven the car down the hill at full speed (thus high-lighting the unnecessary complication of these antiquated controllers, on which the key had to be switched to a braking position and then the handle moved through the ordinary driving positions, to bring the car to a standstill).

The findings were that the accident was due to an error of judgement of an insufficiently experienced driver and the presiding officer pointed out that the consequences were much worse than they need have been, owing to the serious overloading of the car. As a result, the carrying of passengers on the top deck was forbidden on this part of the line for the time being. The driver had been discharged from the army as unfit after a nervous breakdown.

147. Car No. 12 of 1898 descending the lower High Street before widening.   Courtesy Dover Corporation.

An Inquest, drawing similar conclusions, was held on those passengers who lost their lives and the General Manager presented a report to the Tramways Committee on 11th September 1917, in which he praised the assistance rendered to the injured, by the Police, medical men and local people. He also stated that the body of car No. 20 was too much strained to be of any further service. In this respect he was evidently unduly pessimistic, as it was repaired by his successor. This accident cost the Corporation £14,575 in compensation, of which only £1,000 was recoverable from the insurance. It necessitated a 1s. 6d. increase in the Rates.

Change in Management

At this, the worst possible time, the rise in running costs owing to the war, made an increase in fares necessary. (See Fares & Tickets section for further details). To repair some of the worst worn sections of the track, 940 yards of the inward-bound road of the sleeper track on the River line were now lifted and the points at the River terminus, being thus rendered useless, were also taken out.

The River service had now dwindled to one car an hour and the main line service to every ten minutes, but in November 1917 this latter was improved to a 7 minutes headway, using six cars and the hourly through service became a half hourly shuttle from Buckland

148. No. 20 overturned at the bottom of Crabble Road on 19th August 1917. Tramway Museum Society.

to River. Even so the Manager, Mr. Carden had to face some very outspoken criticism, for not only were the services inadequate, but the condition of the track and overhead wiring were deplorable; about half the cars were unserviceable and some of those in use were running on one motor. To all this, Mr. Carden replied that it was not his fault as spare parts were unobtainable.

Nevertheless, Mr. Carden fell ill and was advised to resign on medical grounds, which he did in February 1918. He was succeeded in March by Mr. E. H. Bond, the Electrical Works Superintendent, who had already held appointments with the Isle of Thanet and Colchester Tramways, before coming to Dover in 1915 and consequently as General Manager at Dover, he was able to bring very valuable experience to bear upon the problems confronting him now.

One of Mr. Bond's first measures was to introduce fixed stopping places; another was to obtain a set of steel wheels with removable tyres, so that "flats" could be dealt with more expeditiously than with the cast iron wheels with which Dover had been afflicted for so long. The most urgent task however, was the renewal of the overhead wire, for which purpose, he was obliged to acquire a new tower wagon, the old one being now unfit for use. Practically the whole of the conductor wires were renewed, requiring much night work and over a longer period many of the poles were renewed by ones of plain design without scrollwork and ornamental bases, others were reinforced and the rigid suspension replaced by bowstrings.

In April 1919 the embargo on top deck travel on the River section was lifted, provided that there was no standing on the cars at all, so

Mr. Bond asked the Council to authorize the restoration of the double track, the purchase of three new cars and the provision of workshop facilities at Buckland depot. Even the possibility of constructing an alternative route to River was discussed, as the existing line was not thought to be conveniently placed, but as the Manager put the cost of such a diversion at £35,000, the idea was quickly given up. The Council appear to have agreed to the other three items and a contract was placed for the three new cars costing £6,000, but the new workshops and the track doubling came to nothing.

The new cars, constructed by the English Electric Company Ltd., at Preston and numbered 25-27, were delivered in July 1920 and were similar in appearance to 22-24, but had illuminated destination boxes under the canopy and the headlamp on the dash from the outset. They were pleasant looking cars and painted in an improved emerald green and cream livery. (Earlier in 1920 the Corporation looked into the possibility of purchasing five single deck bodies from English Electric for £6,750, instead, presumably to work the River route).

The manager wisely obtained a good stock of spare parts for these cars and was thus able to maintain them in an excellent condition. As soon as they were got on the road, a through service between River and the Sea Front was introduced using two out of the three cars on a twenty five minute headway, sandwiched in between Buckland cars. This did result in the River cars often duplicating the times of the Buckland cars and after one season the River service was merged with that on the main line, every third car running through. This worked very well except that in wet weather, the River cars taking the double load inside were often overcrowded.

The responsibility for the maintenance of the track rested with the Borough Engineer, who was apt to defer renewals and repairs until the carriage-way required attention. Whilst no doubt this was an economical policy, it was not conducive to efficient operation of the trams, nor to their quiet and smooth running, hence, the Manager more than once asked that this work should be transferred to his own department, without satisfaction. However, quite considerable renewals were carried out in 1920, including King Street, Market Square, Cannon Street, Biggin Street and the junction with Worthington Street, which was reduced to single track. Various other sets of points were renewed and many of those taken out had short tongues like those used on horse tramways.

In July 1921, although much of the track was still in bad condition, the Manager introduced a summer service at reduced headways. Mr. Bond had an ingenious system for working out timetables. He assumed for operational purposes that the three outer town termini were equidistant from Worthington Street, each with a journey time of ten minutes and the same time was allowed between Buckland and River.

The overall scheduled speed was 6.15 miles per hour, including stops; this was low even for a small town, but was not unreasonable considering the narrow streets, with a high proportion of single track and sharp curves. From the summer of 1921, four cars were required on the Maxton line and eight on the main line, four of which had to be suitable for running through to River. Poster timetables were displayed at the principal stopping places, setting out in full the departure times from the termini of each of the three services. Clock dials were fixed at New Bridge, Worthington Street and Buckland, and the crew of each River car altered them to show the time of the next River car. Another dial at River showed the time of the "Next car to Town".

Also in 1921, cars Nos. 1, 8 and 9 were dismantled, the body of No. 1 being used as a waiting room at Buckland and one of the others at Maxton. At the same time, Car No. 20 damaged in the 1917 crash, was rehabilitated.

In March 1921 it was stated that a loss of £11,000 had been made, mainly due to the high cost of power, which was 6d per unit the highest in the country. As the Electricity dept. was also making a heavy loss, little could be done.

Minor derailments and consequent delays were rather frequent during this period owing to the state of the track; but the only really spectacular accident occurred when No. 18, shortly after leaving the stopping place in the Market Square, left the up track and swung right across the road and the down track to finish up on the tar macadam beyond, perilously near a steep camber, but fortunately without serious consequences.

In the Autumn of 1921 the Manager again pressed for the restoration of double track on the River section and also asked for the renewal of the rails on Priory Station Bridge, still equipped with Dicker joints, relaying at Elms Vale Road and the construction of a short new line along Priory Road, to facilitate the transfer of cars to and from Maxton Depot and the introduction of a through service between Buckland and Maxton if desirable; and finally the long planned extension from the "George" corner to the Marine Station, over the new viaduct which was then almost complete, but he met with no success. The Marine Station extension was rejected on the grounds of prohibitive cost and after a delegation had visited York, Leeds and Bradford in March a trial with a trolleybus from Ramsbottom was staged on 6th & 7th July 1922 by the Railless Co., to see if the whole of the Pier section below New Bridge could be converted to this form of transport, together with the River route, the sleeper section of which could then be made up as a proper road. However, the trolleybus which was a primitive single-decker roused no great enthusiasm. In the meantime, more urgent track renewals were carried out, one of which was the alteration of the terminal loop at Maxton to a single track terminus close to the footway outside the "Orange Tree" public house. New doors were supplied for both depots.

In 1923, further plans to replace the trams with trolleybuses met with intense opposition and no more was heard of them for some time. On 21st September 1923, there was another accident on the River route, although fortunately much less serious than the previous one. Car No. 23 got out of control on the gradient leading down from the sleeper track to the "Cricketers Inn" and overran the worn and rickety points of the old crossover, colliding head on with her sister car No. 24, which was waiting at the foot of Crabble Road. As a result two ladies who attempted to get off the car while still moving, received injuries, though not of a serious nature. Again the driver complained of difficulty with the brakes and although one adjusting nut of the hand brake had stripped its thread, the Corporation claimed that otherwise the brakes were in good order. Once again the driver had applied power when imagining that he was applying the electric brakes. In an attempt to save the situation, the driver had driven the car from the rear end and when the matter was reported to the Ministry of Transport, they not unnaturally drew the conclusion that by so doing quite unnecessarily, the driver had only added to his difficulties. It was ruled that only cars fitted with the latest type of braking should be used on the River section, and in practice this meant working it as a shuttle until other cars could be fitted with these brakes. At the same time, it was decided by the Manager that the driver should be transferred to some other employment within the department. As soon as possible after the collision, a new set of points, with left-hand turn out, was put in at the cattle crossing, thus restoring to use the remaining portion of double track beyond the "Cricketers" and en-suring that cars were running on their proper road before reaching the gradient. The old crossover was taken out and replaced by plain track; this work was completed early in 1924.

A suggestion that the Pier-Buckland service should be extended to the top of Crabble Hill for the benefit of the people living at the new Council estate nearby was rejected on the grounds that the necessary crossover would cost £300; but a new 2d. farestage was authorized between that point and the New Bridge. In that year also, 1924, the double track in the High Street, from Biggin Street to the Hospital, was renewed at an estimated cost of £2,450 and the layout was im-proved by straightening up the road where it ran into single track, thus eliminating unnecessary reverse curves.

The Reconditioned Tramcars
Since the end of the war, Mr. Bond had accomplished a great deal towards putting the cars into good working order. No. 17 had been

brought out with normal staircases; Nos. 18, 19, 21, with 22, 23 and 24, by the making up of arrears of maintenance, were in good working order and running sweetly, also the damage to No. 20 had been made good and with new upper deck seating, she was in use on the Buckland-Pier service. The new cars, Nos. 25-27, were of course in excellent condition, while Nos. 15 & 16 were in good order but slow, having been fitted with up to date life guards and the head lamps in the dash. In order to overcome the difficulty in running to River, mentioned in connection with the 1923 accident, Nos. 21 and 22-24 were equipped with DB1-K3B controllers having the rheostatic brakes applied by means of the main handle, and No. 21 also required slipper brakes. When this was done, seven cars were available for the River section and a through service could be restored. These cars were also thoroughly repainted, but Mr. Bond thought that some of the older cars were not worth the expenditure of time and money. On his reporting this to the Council, discussions broke out again about the future of the system and when early in 1925, a large body of railway and government employees at the Pier, petitioned for the extension over the viaduct, but the Council still hesitated. The renewal of the existing line from New Bridge to "The George" corner would cost £7,075; the extension £10,000 and if the system were to be thus perpetuated, the new cars required would cost £5,250. It was therefore suggested that the trams should be cut back to New Bridge and through buses or trolleybuses run to the Marine Station; but the Council at this juncture felt unable to make so far-reaching a decision, and instead, authorized the renewal of the whole of the track below New Bridge and the retention of the existing service to Crosswall, but said nothing about new rolling stock.

However, in April 1925, at the Manager's urgent request, a Sub-Committee, conducted an inspection of the cars and authorized the conversion of the body of No. 2 into a shelter for South Road, River and the expenditure of £200 on the rehabilitation of Nos. 6, 13 and 14. The Manager and his Assistant, Mr. Albert Pollard decided to start on No. 13. They removed the old sagging platforms and built on new ones with higher dashes, canopies and permanent vestibules. The stairs were reconstructed to the direct half-turn pattern; a new trolley mast and boom, together with top deck seating for 26 were provided. The motors and controllers were fully overhauled and the cost of thus reconditioning this one car was £216 3s. The only faults were that the stairs and platforms were somewhat cramped and the lack of funds precluded the modernization of the interior of the car. It was however, given push-button bells.

The "Dover Express" commented very favourably on this conversion, drawing attention at the same time to the very cramped conditions in Maxton Workshop, in which the rebuilding of No. 13 had been carried out, thus reflecting great credit on Messrs. Bond and Pollard, adding "Given a sufficient floor area with some additions in the way of machinery, there seems to be no reason why new car bodies should not be constructed in the tramway works."

In May 1926 the services were interrupted by the General Strike, in which most of the staff took part. By early June, coal shortages necessitated a reduction in service and staff were put on three-quarter time.

Meanwhile, in the autumn, the Council at last gave authority for the renewal of the Pier section of track to begin, and also agreed to the renewal of the Worthington Street junction in the form of a single track curve with a trailing crossover connection to the down line, with a view to running Maxton cars through to the sea front during the summer.

Snargate Street was tackled first and considerable trouble was experienced with sub-surface works, so that the estimated time for this part of the job was exceeded. However, when at length it was finished it was seen to have brought a considerable improvement, especially at Court's Corner, where the very sharp curve close to the footway was very much eased and the superelevation corrected. The points at "The George" corner were also renewed, and although still having a sharp turnout, the layout was much improved.

In Strond Street a new layout was adopted at the terminus, consisting of a straight stub, with the terminal straining post erected almost on the edge of the quay. This new arrangement was carried out at the same time as the erection of a new foot-bridge by the Southern Railway Company, with sloping approaches and leading to Clarence Place; the level crossing was abolished and the adjacent carriageway taken into the railway reservation. The rest of the tramway track was renewed, but to the old layout. Next, work was undertaken at the Worthington Street junction as it was considered undesirable to have the road up at Worthington Street during the summer season, while visitors were about. Although the junction was laid out as already proposed, the overhead wiring was not altered and the Maxton branch wire, was anchored off above the main line wires, to a post on the other side of Biggin St., without making a physical connection, as the idea of a through route from Maxton to the Pier had been given up again. However, for a time, one early morning car on Sundays from Maxton did make a trip up to Buckland and back, to fill in some spare time. This working was rarely attempted at other times, as it meant swinging the trolley pole in a busy street.

When the work below New Bridge was resumed only the two double track sections in Northampton Street, which still had "Dicker" joints, were renewed and naturally this resulted in a considerable reduction of noise.

Second Hand Rolling Stock

We now come to one of the most interesting periods in the history of Dover Corporation Tramways. The Council were impressed with the rehabilitation of car No. 13 and approved the reconditioning of

149. No. 15 as rebuilt without vestibules, in 1927, shown loading at Buckland terminus.

Photo H. Wightman. Courtesy A. J. Watkins.

150. No. 16 as rebuilt with vestibuled platforms, in 1927.   R. Elliott.

Nos. 15 and 16 as well, but in the autumn of 1926 the Manager announced that he still needed new cars; No. 20, the car damaged in the 1917 disaster, was now in a dangerous condition and not worth even converting to a single decker. Mr. Bond, therefore made a search around and on his recommendation the Council authorized the purchase of two secondhand cars from Darlington at a cost of £250 each, including some spare parts and transport costs. These two cars had covered tops with end balconies and roomy vesibuled platforms. They seated 55 in all. They took the numbers 8 and 9 in the Dover fleet and were brought out in the Dover green and ivory livery. At first they emitted a peculiar murmuring noise, but after Mr. Bond had carried out a good deal of work on their motors, they became very popular cars; they were very wide and stocky and their additional capacity in wet weather was appreciated. After a short while both were regularly assigned to the Maxton line.

In January 1927, after a further review of rolling stock, work started on the rebuilding of Nos. 15 and 16, similar to No. 13. Both already had longer platforms than No. 13, but for some reason, No. 15 retained open platforms when rebuilt, however No. 16 had trapezoidal vestibuled platforms. In both cases the seating capacity was increased by the inclusion of canopies and the motors were thoroughly reconditioned, making them both into speedy cars.

However, it was not considered that the rest of the old stock was in a condition worthy of the expense of rebuilding. Therefore, the Manager obtained authority to purchase five more second-hand cars, this time from West Hartlepool, at a total cost of £850. They were not covered topped, as West Hartlepool was not allowed to fit top covers, but in other respects they were modern, with four windows each side and were about 2 ft. 9 ins. longer than any other cars at Dover. They had upholstered cane rattan transverse seats inside for 23 and weatherproof seats with flaps on top. They retained their Hartlepool numbers 1-5 at Dover and also the dark red livery which was found to wear well (except No. 2 which was repainted green). Being open topped yet modern cars, they were considered most suitable for the River service and accordingly were equipped with slipper brakes removed from other Dover cars. As their arrival left the depots overcrowded, authority was obtained to scrap the remaining old cars, Nos. 3, 4, 5, 6, 7, 10, 11, 12 and 14.*

The only major permanent way work in 1927 was the renewal of the single track in the High Street between the Hospital and Tower Hamlets. This was a badly corrugated section and with this relaying, the roadway was lowered about 3 feet to reduce the camber. An evening postal collection by tramcar commenced in July 1928, when

*Apparently No. 6 was not scrapped at once, as Council Minutes record its being involved in an accident on 16th September 1929.

151. No. 4 (ex West Hartlepool) at the foot of Crabble Road near the site of the disaster of 1917. A glimpse of the railway arch over Crabble Road can be seen in the background.

Photo H. Wightman   *courtesy A. J. Watkins*

a collecting box was hung on the dash of the car timed to leave River at 8.30 p.m.

Two more second-hand top covered cars were purchased on 12th December 1928, when the Manager visited the Tividale Works of the Birmingham & Midland Joint Tramways Committee. Of five cars which they were offering for sale, he selected two Nos. 15 & 17, which became Dover Nos. 11 & 12 and the price was £300 each, plus delivery charges. They were high and narrow, with partial vestibules round the front; their design was very plain but they were solidly built and structurally sound. At the same time Mr. Bond purchased three spare top covers at £50 each and these were fitted to Dover cars Nos. 25, 26 and 27. The top deck seats were rearranged with a straight instead of staggered gangway. As well as the two complete cars and three top covers, miscellaneous spare parts to the value of £92 were also acquired. The slipper brakes from Nos. 25-27 were then transferred to West Hartlepool cars, since covered top cars could not run to River. All the covered top cars at Dover had to be fitted with a simple travelling device on the trolley pole, to keep the rope close in to the car, a necessary precaution when the cars passed on loops with side running overhead wires. (See the section on "Power Supply & Current Collection" for further details.)

In September 1929 the Harbour Board announced that they had decided to take in for dock purposes, all the land on the south side of Snargate Street, between "The George" corner and Court's Corner, including the carriageway of Commercial Quay; all property between was to be pulled down. The Corporation was to retain the road materials of Commercial Quay and the Board gave them enough land to widen Snargate Street to 50 feet, together with the sum of £7,000. This would have enabled the Corporation to double the track and eliminate the troublesome blind curves, and there would probably have been something left over with which to buy some new poles; but in fact they only eased the curves and lengthened the passing loop at "The George" corner, so that when the work was completed it was found that the corner was still blind and the signals had to be retained. Moreover the track in Snargate Street was badly out of centre.

In May 1930, the body of car No. 17, the 1902 car was sold for £5 for use as a shelter on a small-holding and the Manager informed the Tramways Committee that the fleet was now reduced to 21 cars, i.e. Nos. 1-5 ex-West Hartlepool, Nos. 8-9 ex-Darlington, Nos. 11-12 ex-B.&M. Joint Committee, Nos. 13, 15 & 16 original cars recondi-tioned, Nos. 18, 19 & 21 of 1905, Nos. 22-24 of 1912 and Nos. 25-27 of 1920, which were top covered in 1929. One of these the Manager said was almost beyond useful service (probably No. 22) and accord-ingly he sought permission to purchase more second-hand cars. By this time the B. & M. Joint Committee had ceased to operate trams and their remaining cars had been put in the hands of a dealer, Messrs. A. Devey & Co. Ltd., but had not been removed from B. & M. premises, where Mr. Bond the Dover Manager called in May 1930. This time he purchased five car bodies, five trucks, six motors and four controllers at a price of £470 for the lot. Together with the transport costs, this came to £800. The cars were similar to Nos. 11-12, but lacked the vestibule fronts. When assembled and put into service at Dover, they were painted in the dark red and ivory livery like the West Hartlepool cars and numbered 6, 7, 10, 14 and 17. Their arrival enabled the manager to relegate to the reserve, all the remaining open top cars except those required for the River service. It was also decided to standardize on the dark red livery and other cars, as renovated, including Nos. 25-27, eventually appeared repainted thus. The ex-B. & M. cars of the second batch had miniature destination boxes under the canopy, against the bulkhead; some spare boxes of this type were acquired with these cars and were then fitted to a number of other Dover cars. When repainted in the red livery, No. 27 received upholstered seats inside, but the materials were of poor quality and did not wear well, consequently the experiment was not repeated on other cars.

152. No. 5 (ex-West Hartlepool) crossing the railway from the George corner into Strond Street. The date is subsequent to the widening of Snargate Street.　　　Photo H. Wightman.　Courtesy A. J. Watkins.

During the winter of 1930/31, the very badly worn track on the town side of Priory Station was at last renewed at a cost of £1,502, but on the farther side, which contained the last of the Dicker joints, the track was not renewed until January 1933.

In September 1931, a new layout was put down at the junction of Biggin Street with High Street, where the double track had been singled in 1900. For many years, the points at the High Street end, had been equal turnout, laid askew as a substitute for a right-hand turnout; this was now rectified and the single track extended about 25 yards further north, thus eliminating the reverse curves. Some patches of rail corrugation were tackled by an outside contractor and several joints welded, evidently with satisfactory results.

In September 1933 car No. 22 had to be scrapped as the body was no longer in a safe condition, and it was thought that Nos. 19 and 21 would not last much longer. Consequently, two complete cars were purchased from Birmingham Corporation, together with two spare bodies, the complete cars costing £190 and the bodies £60 each. They were typical Birmingham four wheelers of the earlier type with three side windows and when the two spare bodies had been provided with trucks and equipment from scrapped Dover cars, the four were numbered 19-22. However one of these cars was required for the River service, so No. 22 was deprived of its top cover and given the trolley mast and other upper deck fittings from the old No. 22. All four cars remained in the Birmingham livery of cobalt blue and cream, so that at this time there could be seen on the Dover system, small as it was, trams in three colours, green, red and blue, also several different styles. The elaborate lettering on the rocker panels ceased to be renewed at about this time.

The Abandonment of the Trams

On 30th April 1934, a new 1d. Fare Stage was introduced between Beaconsfield Road and the top of Crabble Hill, and it might have been thought that such a reform though relatively unimportant, but following the arrival of the numerous second-hand cars in good condition would portend the continuation of tramway operation, but the end was very near. Discussions on future transport policy had been held, on and off, for more than ten years and in this very month the East Kent Road Car Co. Ltd., (the large bus operators in the area), offered to assist by providing services within the Borough. As the Council were unable to arrive at a decision, they called in as an advisor, the General Manager of Birmingham Corporation Transport Department, asking him to report under three heads; (i) the rehabilitation of the tramways (ii) the East Kent offer and (iii) the operation of Corporation buses. Trolleybuses were not contemplated.

To cut a long and painful story short, the following month the Birmingham Manager was empowered to negotiate with the East Kent company. The agreement eventually reached was that the Company would operate buses between the Marine Station, Buckland and River and between Market Square and Maxton; after working expenses had been defrayed and a capitation charge deducted of 3d. per bus-mile, the Corporation would receive three-quarters of the profit. The portion

153. No. 21 (ex-Birmingham Corporation) at Pier (Crosswall).
Photo R. Neale.   Courtesy H. V. Jinks.

306

of the Company's interurban services within the Borough, would be regarded as covered by the same agreement, and finally, the Corporation would have no liability in the event of any loss.

The trams, therefore, ceased running on the night of 31st December 1936, when No. 10 (ex-B. & M.) ran as a ceremonial last car and there were the usual demonstrations. The buses took over the next morning.

The open top trams were driven out onto the sleeper track at River under their own power and there disposed of by burning. The other cars were scrapped by contract. Both depot buildings are still in use for other purposes (June 1972).

For a few months the River service was provided by single deck buses, running by way of Lower Road, while the sleeper track was being made up into a concrete carriageway (as an extension of Lewisham Road, River) after which the service reverted to its original route. The steep portion of Crabble Road was widened and a new railway bridge erected with much greater headroom than the old brick arch; then double deck covered top buses took over the River service. Over the many years which have now elapsed since the Dover trams ceased to operate, there have of course been many changes in the bus services, but they are still provided by "East Kent".

The only part of the former tramway system not served by buses is Strond Street, as the buses now go over the viaduct to reach the Marine Station. The buses also reach out to Kearsney and a number of other housing estates beyond the tram termini. In recent years a system of one way streets, has been introduced between New Bridge and Buckland Bridge, following the tram route northbound.

The Sea Front Railway

We cannot close without a brief mention of the Sea Front Railway, which was constructed in 1917 for the transport of war materials to the Naval Dockyard at East Cliff. It was of standard gauge and made a trailing connection with the Prince of Wales Pier line (already mentioned in connection with the tram crossing at The George Corner). Trains had to run from the Folkestone or Marine Station direction towards the Pier and reverse to get onto the sea front line and therefore normally required two locomotives, one at each end. The line ran along the sea front close to the Promenade but about two hundred yards at each end were fenced, where the carriageway was narrow. Near the India Monument (New Bridge) there was a run round loop.

After the war, with the abandonment of the Naval Dockyard, the whole line was transferred to the Harbour Board and for some years the East Cliff yards were used for breaking up scrapped vessels, the naval fuel tanks were leased to Shell-Mex and arrangements were made for shipping Kent coal from the Eastern Arm. In spite of strong local objection, considerable use was made of the Sea Front railway,

154. Car No. 19 on the private track of the River line, passing Crabble
Athletic Ground.   Courtesy Ray Warner.
155. Row of open top cars, No. 23 leading, dumped on the private track
to River, after the closure.   Tramway Museum Society.

but when the fences were removed, all trains had to be preceded by a
man with a red flag. Small South Eastern & Chatham 0-6-0 tank
engines of the P Class were generally used on this line.

After the second world war a spur was laid connecting the Sea Front
railway directly to the Western Docks line and eliminating the need
to reverse (a move facilitated by the destruction of a number of dwelling houses by enemy action.) However, the shipment of coal ceased

as did the ship-breaking and eventually the movement of oil amounted to one tank wagon daily; as this could then be undertaken by road, the last train ran on the 31st December 1964 and much of the track had been lifted by 1967.

156. One of the original batch of cars with a Blackwell's "Patent Swivelling Arm" trolleymast as first fitted.

Tramway Museum Society.

Rolling Stock

(a) Original Cars

Nos. 1-10. Bodies built by — BRUSH ELECTRICAL ENGINEER-ING CO LTD., at Loughborough in 1897.

Dimensions — Saloon 15′ 0″ long, 6′ 4″ wide, 25′ 8″ over platforms.

Seating — 20 inside, 24 outside. Direct quarter-turn stairs.

Electrical Equipment supplied by — DICK, KERR & CO. LTD.

Two American G.E.800 motors of 25 horse power each. Two G.E.C. K2 controllers.

Truck — PECKHAM "Cantilever" 6′ 0″ wheelbase.

Braking — Hand and rheostatic.

These cars were of the short canopy type usual at this early date and had five side windows with curved tops and ventilation slits above, leading to an internal clerestorey, with the bowed hoop sticks exposed. Two cars, probably Nos. 3 & 10 were supplied as trailers without electrical equipment and lacking the metal decency boards on the upper deck; they were motorized within the year.

157. Nos. 15 and 16 (1899) outside Maxton depot. Note outside springs of trolley standards. *Courtesy H. V. Jinks.*

A large electric headlamp was mounted on the short canopy roof and the cars had low dashes with the controllers and hand brake staffs protruding well above them. Large folding spring steel "Providence" life guards were carried until about 1902. Blackwell's "Patent Swivelling Arm" trolley masts were carried on the upper deck, well offset to one side. These which had previously only been used at Leeds, were the first design to have internal springs, but were tall and slender with the spring enclosed in a peculiar circular box at the top. The wheels in the swivel trolley-heads were of the "West End" type. Dover is said to have been the first undertaking to equip its cars with current consumption meters, which they carried for the first few years.

The arched ceiling, small bulkhead windows, high-waisted doors and dark mahogany woodwork in the saloon combined to give a dark interior to these cars.

The rheostatic braking was of a very early type on which the controller handle had to be brought back to the "Off" position, the key moved to a special "Braking" position before the braking notches could be applied; a complicated arrangement which the 1917 and 1923 accidents showed that a driver in panic was incapable of mastering.

The saloon seats were longitudinal and upholstered in red Utrecht velvet, while the reversible upper deck seats, which were staggered two and one about the centre, had wooden turn-over flaps to present a dry surface after rain.

All these cars had wooden blocks as collision fenders and coupling gear was fitted until Nos. 3 & 10 had been motorized. Nos. 8 & 9 were canibalized for spares in 1918 and No. 2 was converted to a waiting room in 1925. The rest were withdrawn between 1927 and 1929.

Nos. 11-14. Bodies built by GEORGE F. MILNES & CO. LTD., of Birkenhead in 1898.

Dimensions — Saloon 15' 0" long, 6' 0" wide. 25' 0" overall length.

Seating 20 inside, 24 outside. Direct quarter turn stairs.

Electrical equipment supplied by DICK, KERR & CO. LTD. (Through B.T-H.)

Two Walker 33N motors of 25 horse power each.

Two Walker S.7 controllers.

Truck — PECKHAM Cantilever, 6' 0" wheelbase.

Braking — Hand & rheostatic.

Nos. 11-12 were supplied early in 1898 and Nos. 13-14 later in the year. These cars were generally similar to Nos. 1-10, but there were detailed differences in body design. For example the head lamps on the canopy were further to the left when viewed from the front, there were smaller ventilator slits over the windows, light angle section steel collision fenders were fitted instead of wooden bumpers and coupling gear was provided. Moreover, the number was applied in the centre of the dash instead of well over to one side as on Nos. 1-10. These cars had "Providence" liefguards from the start. They cost £713 each. They had Blackwell outside spring trolleymasts, shorter than those of Nos. 1-10. (illustrated on pages 290 & 291).

In April 1904, No. 14 was fitted with an experimental top cover over the saloon supplied by Milnes, Voss & Co. but new regulations introduced in 1905, necessitated its removal then.

No. 13 was rebuilt in 1926 at a cost of £216-3-0d. The top deck was extended over the platforms to form canopies with seating, while new higher dashes and glass vestibule windscreens were fitted. The only fault was that No. 13 had very short platforms and they were not lengthened. Half turn spiral staircases were provided and a hinged opening ventilator was made in the centre window of the saloon. The motors and controllers were thoroughly reconditioned at the same time. No. 13 remained in existence to the end, but Nos. 11, 12 & 14 were scrapped in 1927.

Nos. 15-16. Bodies built by J.G. BRILL & CO. of Philadelphia, U.S.A. in 1898.

Dimensions — Saloon 16' 0" long, 6' 0" wide. Overall length 27' 0".

Seating 20 inside, 24 outside. Direct quarter turn stairs.

Electrical equipment supplied by — DICK, KERR & CO. LTD.

Two WALKER 33N motors of 25 horse power each.

Two WALKER S.7 controllers.

Truck — BRILL 21.E (made in U.S.A.) Wheelbase 6' 0".

Braking — Hand & rheostatic.

As suitable bodies were evidently unobtainable in Great Britain at the time, Dick Kerr placed this order with Brill & Co. in the U.S.A. on 9th June 1898 and they were promised for 10th September. They were generally similar to the earlier cars, but more substantially constructed and differed in many details, such as the shape of the ventilation slits, which even extended right round the very short canopies. They had proper internal clerestories and higher dashes, fitted to longer platforms. These cars had stout channel type collision fenders, but as delivered, still had coupling gear. The saloon doors were double, parting in the middle and the railings round the upper deck were higher than on the earlier cars, with a narrow strip of wire netting between them. A similar car was exhibited by Brill at the London Aquarium in 1897.

Both Nos. 15 and 16 were rebuilt in 1927, similarly to No. 13, but as they already had slightly longer platforms, the overall result was more satisfactory. For some reason, however, No. 15 was not provided with vestibule windscreens, but No. 16 received trapezoidal or hexagonal dashes with glass windscreens, in which the front window was made to open. With reconditioned motors, these became quite fast and useful cars, but they saw little service after the arrival of the full complement of secondhand cars. (illustrated as rebuilt on page 301).

No. 17.   Body built by ELECTRIC RAILWAY & TRAMWAY CARRIAGE WORKS LTD., Preston, 1902.
Dimensions — Saloon 16′ 0″ long, 6′ 3″ wide. Overall length 27′ 6″.
Seating 22 inside, 26 outside. Reversed stairs.
Electrical Equipment supplied by — DICK, KERR & CO. LTD.
Two DK.33N motors of 25 horse power each.
Two DK. type S.7 controllers.
Truck — BRILL 21.E 6′ 0″ wheelbase.
Braking — Hand and rheostatic.

This was the first car acquired with the later traditional style of body, with three windows each side, opening glass vents above and canopies with seats extending over the platforms. There were double doors to the saloon, parting in the middle. It was the only car at Dover to have reversed stairs and they were exchanged for the normal half turn variety in 1918. At the same time the headlamp, formerly on the upper deck, was moved to the centre of the dash, regardless of the rather large fleet number then painted there and the tops of the figures peered above the lamp. This car had a more modern trolley mast with internal springs.

It was withdrawn in 1930 and the body sold for use as a shed.

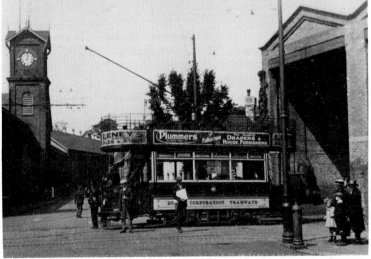

158. Upper—The illusive No. 17 outside Buckland Depot, in its original condition. The only Dover car with reversed stairs.

Courtesy Ray Warner.

159. Lower—No. 19 entering Buckland Depot, with the track continuing past the paper mill towards River.

Courtesy "Len's of Sutton".

313

Nos. 18-21. Bodies built by UNITED ELECTRIC CAR CO. LTD., (Successors to E.R. & T.C.W. Ltd.), Preston in 1905.

Dimensions — Saloon 16′ 0″ long, 6′ 3″ wide. 27′ 6″ overall length.

Seating — 22 inside, 26 outside. Half-turn normal spiral stairs.

Electrical equipment supplied by DICK, KERR & CO. LTD.

Two DK.33N motors of 25 horse power each.

Two D.K. type S.7 controllers. (No. 21 had DB.1-K.3B after 1920.)

Truck — BRILL 21.E. 6′ 0″ wheelbase.

Braking — Hand, rheostatic and Spencer track brakes.

These four cars were ordered on 22nd February 1905 at a cost of £575 each. They were generally similar to No. 17, with double opening saloon doors, but had normal half turn stairs. There was scroll work at the back end of the dash under the stairs. As they were intended for use on the River service, they were delivered with "Spencer" track brakes, actuated by a large brass wheel concentric with the handbrake staff. They had Dick, Kerr trolley masts with internal springs, type TS.8. These cars had fixed double seats on the canopy, but when No. 20 was repaired after a serious accident in 1917, it received a curved seat on each canopy. It was scrapped in 1926 and Nos. 18, 19 and 21 in 1933.

Nos. 22-24. Bodies built by BRUSH ELECTRICAL ENGINEER-ING CO. LTD. at Loughborough in 1912.

Dimensions — Saloon 16′ 0″ long, 6′ 6″ wide. 28′ 0″ over platforms.

Seating — 22 inside, 26 outside. Half-turn spiral stairs.

Electrical equipment supplied by BRITISH THOMSON-HOUSTON LTD.

Two B.T-H motors of 35 horse power each.

Two G.E.C. K.10 controllers. (Dick, Kerr D.B.1 K.3B after 1924.)

Truck — BRILL 21.E of 6′ 6″ wheelbase.

Braking — Hand, rheostatic and Spencer track brakes.

These cars were generally similar to Nos. 18-21, but had a number of detailed differences, related to the special design features of each manufacturer. The tumble-home of the rocker panel was more pronounced and they had the typical Brush pointed cutaway on the corner posts of the saloon. The seats at the ends of the canopy were curved and as built the headlamps were located on the canopy bends, but were later removed to the dash. They had no destination equipment, except for transparent plates hung from the underside of the canopy just above the driver's head and inscribed "RIVER"; they could be

160. No. 22 leaving Buckland Depot. Note hole in front canopy where head lamp had been and small ex-B. & M. destination box on bulkhead.   M. J. O'Connor.

covered when not in use. Proper destination boxes were fitted to No. 24 in 1926.

They were the first cars at Dover to have steel tyred instead of cast iron wheels. They appear to have been more strongly built than Nos. 18-21 and ran very well. There was wire mesh occupying the lower half of the space between the decency board and the top deck railing of these cars. Car No. 22 was scrapped in 1933 when replaced by a second-hand car, but Nos. 23 & 24 were in existence to the end, although little used after 1933.

Nos. 25-27.   Bodies built by ENGLISH ELECTRIC CO. LTD. at Preston in 1920. (Successors of E.R. & T.C.W. Ltd. and U.E.C. Ltd.).

Dimensions — Saloon 16′ 0″ long, 6′ 6″ wide. Length over platforms 28′ 0″.

Seating — 22 inside, 26 outside. Half-turn spiral stairs.

Electrical equipment supplied by — ENGLISH ELECTRIC CO. LTD.

Two D.K.30B motors of 40 horse power each.

Two D.K. D.B.1 Form K3 controllers (without notch regulators).

Truck — ENGLISH ELECTRIC "PRESTON" type of 7′ 6″ wheelbase.

Braking — Hand, rheostatic and "Spencer" track brakes.

These cars were ordered on 31st July 1919 and delivered in July 1920. They were again of the traditional pre-war open top three

315

161. Car No. 26 of 1920 in its original condition at the Pier. Note position of the Dick-Kerr trolley mast close to the upper deck railings, and the absence of a side life guard.　　　　　　　J. V. Horn.

window design and closely similar in appearance to Nos. 18-21 and 22-24, but had steel channel underframes. All seating was in wooden slats, those on the canopies being curved. Pillars and rails were in oak and the interior of the saloon was French polished. The headlamp was on the dash but was not inset and protruded on a metal boss. The TS.8 type trolley mast had a circular contact so that the pole could be turned through a complete circle if necessary. Illuminated destination boxes were fixed under the canopy edge and the cars were fitted with three-slat Hudson & Bowring lifeguards; they also had Phillipson side lifeguards under the offside of the platforms. The wirework round the upper deck, filled the whole of the space between the decency panel and the top rail. The trucks were longer than those under the previous cars.

The only major alteration to these cars occurred in 1928, when they were fitted with top covers. The three spare covers acquired from the B. & M. Joint Committee were of the same length and width as the saloons of these cars and fitted the upper decks without difficulty. They had four side windows, as compared with the three in the lower

162. Upper—No. 26 after fitting with a top cover, at Buckland Bridge.
Late Dr. Hugh Nicol.

163. Lower—No. 8 ex-Darlington at Maxton terminus in 1926.
Late Dr. Hugh Nicol.

saloon and the seating had to be rearranged; the covers put on Nos. 25 & 26 had the usual B. & M. wing window one side at each end, but the one on No. 27 did not. With top covers these cars could no longer run to River and therefore, gave up their slipper brakes to three of the West Hartlepool cars.

(b). **Second-hand Cars.**

Nos. 1-5.   Purchased from West Hartlepool Corporation in 1927. Bodies built by UNITED ELECTRIC CAR CO. LTD. of Preston in 1913.

Dimensions — Saloon 18′ 0″ long, 6′ 4⅛″ wide, 29′ 6″ over platforms.

Seating — 23 inside, 35 outside. Normal half-turn stairs.

Electrical equipment supplied by DICK, KERR & CO. LTD.

Two D.K.20 motors of 30 horse power each.

Two Dick Kerr DB.1-K3.B Controllers.

Truck — U.E.C. "Preston" flexible axle, 8′ 0″ wheelbase.

Braking — Hand and rheostatic. (Spencer slipper brakes fitted at Dover).

These were "second generation" open top cars acquired from West Hartlepool, where because the narrow gauge tram line ran along the sea front, covered tops were not permitted. One car appears to have been purchased as incomplete. They had four windows each side with opening vents above the hexagonal vestibuled dashes on which the front window opened slightly. Except for those in the corners, the lower saloon seats were reversible and arranged two and one; they were of the "Triumph" type upholstered in cane rattan. The inside finish of the saloon was in oak with millboard lining to the roof. The saloon doors were slightly offset to accord with the seating arrangement. "Challenger" dry reversible seats were provided on the upper deck but those above the stairwell were fixed and arranged in conjunction with a draught excluder. Dick Kerr type trolley masts were very much offset to one side and there was a large destination box above the wire screens at each end, with bullseye lenses at the back to illuminate the upper deck. Appropriate blinds were fitted at Dover, but at a later date, the boxes were removed from No. 1, which then received miniature blinds in the glazed openings above the front vestibule windows. Push-button air controlled signal bells were fitted at Dover.

On arrival at Dover No. 2 was repainted in the green livery, but the others retained their dark red and ivory livery, which was found to wear well and set a new standard at Dover. They also retained their Hartlepool numbers. Being intended for the River route they were fitted with track brakes taken from other Dover cars, including 25-27. (These cars illustrated on pages 303 & 305).

Nos. 8-9.   Purchased from Darlington Corporation Light Railways in 1926. Bodies built by UNITED ELECTRIC CAR CO. LTD. of Preston in 1913.

Dimensions — Saloon 16′ 0″ long, 6′ 6″ wide. 28′ 0″ over platforms.

Seating 22 inside, 33 outside. Normal half-turn spiral stairs.

Electrical equipment supplied by SIEMENS & Co.

Two Siemens motors.

Two Siemens controllers (replaced by others at Dover).

Truck — U.E.C. "Preston" flexible wheelbase. 8′ 0″ wheelbase.

Braking — Hand and rheostatic.

These were the only covered top cars owned by Darlington Corporation and had carried their numbers 16 and 17. They had wide bodies with wide angular vestibuled platforms with open canopies above. Apart from earlier experiments with No. 14, these were the first covered top cars to run at Dover. Being built by the same manufacturer as Nos. 1-5 and at about the same time, both classes had a number of features in common, including the shape of the vestibules and the combined seat and draught excluder at the head of the stairs. However, they had wooden longitudinal seats inside and staggered two and one seats in the upper saloon. Their overall height was 15′ 3½″.

When first put into service at Dover, they were rather noisy and a good deal of work had to be done on their motors, electrical equipment and wheels before they could run reliably, but when this had been done, they proved very popular cars.

Originally they had large destination boxes above the upper deck end wire screens, but later on both cars they were replaced by miniature blinds in the glazed opening above the front screen, as on No. 1. On arrival they were repainted from Darlington blue into the full Dover green livery, but towards the end they were painted dark red.

Nos. 11-12. Purchased from the Birmingham & Midland Joint Tramways Committee in 1928.

Bodies built in the B. & M.J.C's own works at Tividale in 1915.

Dimensions — Saloon 16′ 0″ long, 6′ 3″ wide. 28′ 0″ over platforms.

Seating — 22 inside, 26 outside. Normal half-turn spiral stairs.

Electrical equipment — probably reconditioned from stock.

Two G.E. 248 B T-H. motors of 40 horse power each.

Two (unknown) reconditioned controllers.

Truck — B. & M.J.C. "Tividale" 8′ 6″ wheelbase.

Braking — Hand and rheostatic.

Dover Corporation minutes report that these cars had been B. & M. Nos. 15 & 17 and from photographs it is probable that No. 15 became

320

No. 11 at Dover and 17 became 12. They were high narrow cars with four windows each side, each with two hinged opening vents above. There were plain longitudinal seats inside and reversible seats on the upper deck, which had four windows each side to match the lower deck, but in drop frames. In common with many other B. & M. cars, No. 12 had an extra wing window on top one side at each end, but No. 11 did not have this feature. Interior woodwork of the saloons was plain and undecorated. Compared with other cars at Dover, these were very strongly built but heavy and inclined to be noisy.

These two cars had partial vestibules on the front of the dash, with three panes of glass, but the dashes were open at the sides. The glass did not come down to the dash top rail and the space required for the sweep of the hand brake and controller handle was closed by a protruding pressed metal "blister" which G. L. Gundry has compared to a "middle age spread". The Tividale" trucks were longer than anything used previously at Dover, and on arrival No. 12 was fitted with truss rods. (No. 11 had wooden laths instead.)

The B. & M. livery was dark green and yellowish cream and No. 11 was only partially repainted at first, but No. 12 appeared in the full Dover green and ivory livery. As delivered, they did not have destination equipment, but when some other similar ex-B. & M. cars were acquired later q.v., the Manager obtained miniature boxes for these cars as well.

Nos. 6, 7, 10,

14 & 17.   Purchased from A. Devey & Co., Birmingham in 1930. ex-Birmingham & Midland Joint Tramways Committee. Bodies built by BRUSH ELECTRICAL ENGINEER-ING CO. LTD. in 1904. (Rebuilt in 1915).

(except No. 14 built new in 1913 at Tividale, similar to Nos. 11 & 12.)

Dimensions — Saloon 16′ 0″ long, 6′ 3″ wide. Overall length 28′ 0″.

Seating — 22 inside, 27 outside. Normal half turn stairs.

Electrical Equipment — probably reconditioned from stock.

Motors — probably G.E.248, 40 horse power.

Controllers — probably reconditioned from stock.

Truck — B. & M.J.C. "Tividale" fabricated in own works. 8′ 6″ wheelbase.

Braking — Hand and rheostatic.

164.   Upper—No. 12, windscreened car ex-Birmingham & Midland Committee at Buckland Bridge.
165.   Centre—No. 14 of the same type but lacking a windscreen, photographed at the same spot as No. 12.
166.   Lower—No. 6, one of the earlier ex-B. & M. cars as fitted with a top cover, at Maxton terminus.

                All three photos by late Dr. Hugh Nicol.

These cars differed from Nos. 11 & 12 not only in lacking vestibule fronts, as the temporary ones which they had carried were removed before they left Birmingham, but except for No. 14, they were rebuilds of older cars, fitted with top covers. They could be distinguished from Nos. 11, 12 and 14 by the four small air-extractor ventilators in the cantrail and the fact that there was only one hinged opening light, divided into two panes of glass, over each saloon window. In fact all these ex-B. & M. cars differed from one another in detail. Nos. 10 and 14 had the wing windows on the upper deck balconies, while Nos. 6 & 17 had narrow Brush type wire screens on the canopies and the others had plain wire screens extending the full depth from the top rail to the decency board.

The original Brush trucks had been replaced by ones of longer wheelbase fabricated from parts at the B. & M. Tividale Works. Those under Nos. 6 & 14 retained the wide Lycett & Conaty axle boxes and all were fitted at Dover with truss-rods.

Like the other two cars they were strongly built, but again were rather noisy, particularly Nos. 14 & 17. As five bodies, five trucks, six motors and four controllers were bought from Devey, it is probable that the balance of necessary equipment was taken from scrapped Dover cars, and since there is no guarantee that the cars as reassembled at Dover each contained parts all taken from the same B. & M. car, it has not been possible to quote B. & M. numbers.

When put into service at Dover, these cars were painted in a dark red and ivory livery similar to the ex-Hartlepool cars. They had miniature destination boxes on the saloon bulkhead beside the doorway, where although not conspicuous, they evidently met with approval at Dover and spares purchased with these cars appeared on other Dover cars.

Nos. 19-22. Purchased from Birmingham Corporation Tramways in 1933.

Bodies built by UNITED ELECTRIC CAR CO. LTD. at Preston in 1905/06.

Dimensions — Saloon 16′ 0″ long, 6′ 3″ wide, 27′ 6″ overall length.

Seating — 22 inside, 27 outside. Normal half-turn spiral stairs.

Electrical equipment supplied by DICK, KERR & CO. LTD.

Two DK.25.B motors of 25/27 horse power.

Two DK.D1.G, Form G.1 controllers.

Truck — BRILL 21.E, 6′ 0″ wheelbase (as from Birmingham).

Braking — Hand, rheostatic and Westinghouse or Maley magnetic track brakes.

Two complete cars and two spare bodies were purchased from Birmingham Corporation; the spare bodies were provided with trucks and equipment taken from Dover cars recently scrapped. They came from the 21-70 & 221-300 class supplied to Birmingham in 1905. Unfortunately the actual Birmingham fleet numbers are not known. They started life as open top cars with three windows each side and were fitted with top covers between 1911 and 1925. These matched the lower saloon with three windows and like some of the B. & M. cars they had wing windows over the canopies at one side each end. All four had longitudinal wooden seats in the saloon. Full vestibule fronts were fitted to the platforms between 1923 and 1928, with a metal pressing at the bottom of the nearside pane to accommodate the sweep of the brake handle. The two spare bodies mounted on Dover trucks became Nos. 19 and 20, while a complete Birmingham car became No. 21. (illustrated on page 306).

Dover's existing No. 22 was now in a collapsing condition and unfit for further service, thus another car was urgently required for the River service; consequently the remaining ex-Birmingham car had its top cover removed* and replaced by the trolley mast, decency panels, wire netting etc., from the old No. 22, which was then scrapped and the Birmingham car took its number, thus making the series of ex-Birmingham cars Nos. 19-22. Nos. 21 and 22 retained the magnetic track brakes, which in the case of the latter were suitable for use on the River section.

These cars were all in very good condition and retained the Birmingham livery of cobalt blue and cream. They ran well, particularly those on Dover trucks, which probably came from the old Nos. 19 & 21 and were slightly longer than the ex-Birmingham trucks. Nos. 19, 20 and 21 normally operated on the Maxton route, but sometimes ran to Buckland.

Water Car.

Council Minutes show that an order for this car was placed on 5th April 1900, but no mention of it has been found in the records of any British or American tramcar builder. It is possible however, that it was built by Dick, Kerr & Co. of Kilmarnock, whose records for these early days are incomplete.

When delivered it was used for track cleaning in place of the special equipment, formerly carried on an ordinary passenger car. No doubt it was also used for street spraying and snow clearance. It did not receive a fleet number: no photograph of it appears to have survived and it was little used after 1918.

---

*It is recorded in "Modern Tramway" for April 1971, that Arthur G. Wells saw a double deck tram on a lorry stuck under a bridge in Canterbury in 1930s. Presumably this was on its way to Dover and if damaged might have been the one which became No. 22 and would account for why the top cover was not put to some use at Dover.

It appears to have been disposed of by 1927.

Livery of Cars

(a). *1897-1920.* The main colours were medium green and ivory, the former was applied to the dashes, waist panels, stair stringers and trolley mast. The rocker panels, window frames, cant rails, stair risers interior of dash, scrollwork above the toolbox at the corner of the dash and the visible parts of the platform bearers were ivory. The green parts were lined in gold and the car's number also in gold shaded (red?) was on 1-10 well offset to the nearside of the dash. As delivered, Nos. 18-21 had it repeated on both sides. Later the number was hand painted in very large figures in the centre of the dash. There was a single green line on the rocker panel, with key patterns in the corners and dividing it into three panels. The title of the undertaking appeared in small letters in the bottom right hand corner.

Presumably the trucks and lifeguards (excepting the "Providence" spring steel guards) were the usual oxide brown and the controllers, bumpers and hand rails black.

(b). *1920-1927.* The new cars delivered in 1920 appeared in a new and improved livery, in which the dashes, stair stringers, waist panels and cantrails were bright emerald green, the dash and waist panels being lined in gold with floral patterns in each corner, while the cantrail and stair stringer were lined in yellow. The number on the dash and the full title "Dover Corporation Tramways" now appearing on the rocker panel were in gold shaded red. The trolley mast was plain green.

The rocker panels, window frames and decency boards were in ivory lined green. The underside of the canopy was also ivory. The interior of the dash and of the decency boards, together with the stair risers were buff, but later altered to red. Trucks and lifeguards were oxide red, while the collision fenders, controllers and hand rails remained black. The wire mesh around the upper deck on some cars was painted aluminium. On acquisition the ex-Darlington cars, ex-Hartlepool No. 2 and ex-B. & M. No. 12 were painted in this livery. No. 11 was later.

(c). *1927-1933.* The ex-Hartlepool cars Nos. 1-5 arrived painted in a dark red and ivory livery, which was found to wear well and except for No. 2 mentioned above, they remained thus. There was gold lining on the red parts and black lining on the ivory. The full Dover lettering and coat of arms replaced those of West Hartlepool. B. & M. cars Nos. 6, 7, 10, 14 and 17 were repainted in this style before going into service at Dover.

(d). *1933-1937.* When ex-Birmingham Corporation cars Nos. 19-22 arrived they were still painted in that undertaking's livery of cobalt blue and cream, which they retained at Dover, only the number and coat of arms being altered. They had a plain black line on the rocker panel with the name of the undertaking in inch high letters on the right-hand bottom corner of the panel. This arrangement gave a firmer appearance to the saloon and was adopted at Dover. The metal scrollwork round the ends of the upper decks of the Birmingham cars were later painted silver and the trolley mast of No. 22 was green, but otherwise they were not repainted, so that towards the end the blue became almost black. However, as other cars were repainted from this time on, they appeared in the dark red and ivory livery, with yellow lining on the red and plain black lining on the ivory, with the title and manager's name in small letters in the corners, of the rocker panel. Cars which finished up in this style included Nos. 2, 8, 9, and 25-27, also probably others. After a time the dark red faded to dull reddish brown.

The badge used on Dover trams was not a proper coat of arms, but a device made up from three official seals. However, it looked quite unusual and attractive.

Miscellaneous Items

(a). *River Cars.* — Cars used on the River service required certain special features, including track brakes. At first, when the route opened, all cars were fitted with Spencer type track brakes (as already described in the Maidstone Chapter). After the war, this type of brake was only fitted to cars actually used on the River service. The first eight cars arrived fitted with tall slender Blackwell "Patent Swivelling Arm" trolley masts. They proved unsatisfactory and may have been too tall to pass under the bridge in Crabble Road. By the time the River route opened they were to be found on cars Nos. 1, 3, 4, 5, 8, 9, 11 & 12; they were replaced by shorter more modern masts. The other early cars had Blackwell "Dawson" outside spring masts of normal height and later cars had Dick, Kerr "TS.8" or B.T-H "B.1" masts with enclosed springs, on all of which except those on cars 25-27 there was a stop which prevented them from being turned the full circle. Later masts were placed centrally on the roof.

(b). *Life Guards.* — The first cars were delivered with only a fixed wire tray at the ends of the truck, but were quickly fitted with "Providence" spring steel guards against the bottom of the dash. The one at the rear had to be folded up. After 1899, some cars had an intermediate form of guard comprising a metal gate with upright slats. Later Wilson & Bennett life guards with wire mesh gates and trays were used.

The three 1920 cars were the first to have the "Hudson & Bowring" life guard with the gate and tray composed of wooden slats and of a type which soon became practically standard throughout Great Britain. They were henceforth fitted to Dover cars as overhauled. Additionally Nos. 25-27 and the ex-Birmingham Corporation cars had "Phillipson" side life guards under the nearside of the platforms. These were liable to damage and were later replaced by a single thick lath. On some cars, e.g. Nos. 8, 9, 26 & 27, the laths of the gate were replaced by metal rods.

(c). *Destination equipment.* — As Dover operated two self contained routes, the cars were not at first provided with any destination equipment.

From 1904, small boards were hung on the front of the dash and with the introduction of the River service, this arrangement was retained for the new cars, but the uncanopied cars carried a small box beside the headlamp, which when opened in front, revealed the word "RIVER" in black letters on a white ground glass plate, illuminated at the back. Nos. 22-24 had transparent plates lettered "RIVER" hung under the canopy edge, which could be covered when necessary. Nos. 25-27 were delivered with proper destination boxes with illuminated blinds, hung under the canopy edge and similar boxes were latter fitted to No. 24. When the second batch of ex-B. & M. cars arrived, they had miniature destination boxes under the canopy just above the nearside bulkhead window, where they could only be seen properly by passengers in the act of boarding. Nevertheless, Dover acquired a number of these boxes, spare, with the cars and fitted them to several other cars, including Nos. 11-12, 19-23 and even No. 24 eventually lost its larger boxes in favour of a pair of these! Special small blinds were made to fit them. Large blind on Nos. 1-5, 25-28 (and 8-9 at first):—

Large blind	Miniature blinds:
PIER	PIER
BUCKLAND	BUCKLAND
TOP CRABBLE HILL	RIVER
RIVER	MAXTON
SEA FRONT	WORTHINGTON ST.
WORTHINGTON ST.	SEA FRONT
PRIORY STATION	SPECIAL
MAXTON	
SPECIAL CAR	

Miniature blinds were also used in the revised position on Nos. 1, 8 & 9.

Advertising on Cars.

From the beginning, metal plate advertisements were carried on the decency panels at the sides of the upper deck and on the end panels behind the headlamp. In the early days, this latter position was almost invariably occupied by a brown and yellow "LENEY'S ALE & STOUT" advertisement. Later this position was often occupied by the well known blue, white & yellow "BOVRIL", yellow "KENT MESSENGER" or "HAWKESFIELD COAL" advertisements. Like the Thanet system, J. W. Courtenay & Co. was the advertising contractor. The enamelled iron plates continued to be used on the canopies of the upper deck throughout the life of the tramways, but in later years, those on the sides tended to be replaced by paper displays, such as "WHITBREAD'S ALE" etc.

There were "Transparency" advertisements on the opening vents above the saloon windows, which themselves often carried various notices. In later years, paper slips proclaiming current entertainment events were pasted onto the collision fenders and a few cars had advertisement panels on the dash corners.

Services

For the period up to the end of the first world war no exact information is available. From then until the summer of 1920 services were as follows:

Weekdays

Dep. Buckland for Pier and Maxton for Worthington Street 5.28 a.m. and about every 21 minutes until between 7.30 and 8; then as follows:

Service interval 7 minutes; round trip Buckland 42 minutes, Maxton 21 minutes; 6 cars and 3 cars respectively.

Late evenings: service interval 10 minutes, round trip Buckland 40 minutes, Maxton 20 minutes; 4 and 2 cars.

River and Buckland: Service interval 25 minutes; 1 car. (No early morning service).

Sundays

Dep. Buckland for Pier and Maxton for Worthington Street 10.20 a.m. and every 40 minutes until noon, thence every 10 minutes on both routes as late evening service above.

River and Buckland: No Sunday morning service. Afternoons and evenings half-hourly.

Summer 1920

River and Sea Front only: service interval 25 minutes; round trip 50 minutes; 2 cars. Sunday River service uncertain. Other services as above.

Winter 1920/1
Weekdays

Early morning services as above.

Business hours

Buckland and Pier: Service interval 7 minutes (including through River cars), round trip 42 minutes; 6 cars (including 2 River cars).

Maxton and Worthington Street: Service interval 7 minutes, round trip 21 minutes; 3 cars.

Pier and River: Service interval 21 minutes; round trip 63 minutes; 3 cars.

Late evening

Pier and Buckland: Service interval 10 minutes (including through River cars); round trip 40 minutes; 4 cars (including 2 River cars).

327

Pier and River: Service interval 20 minutes, round trip 60 minutes; 3 cars.

Maxton and Worthington Street: Service interval 10 minutes, round trip 20 minutes; 2 cars.

Sundays

Dep. Buckland for Pier and Maxton for Worthington St. 10.20 a.m. and every 20 minutes until 12 noon; thence as late evening weekday service, including, on main line, through River cars.

Pier and River: Service interval 30 minutes; round trip 60 minutes; 2 cars. No Sunday morning service. Ten-minute layover for certain Buckland cars at Buckland to avoid duplicating incoming River car.

Summer 1921
Weekdays

As above (winter 1920/21) until about 11.30 a.m. Then:

Buckland and Pier: Service interval 5 and 6 minutes alternately; (including through River cars); round trip 44 minutes; 8 cars (including 3 River cars).

Maxton and Worthington Street: Service interval 5 and 6 minutes alternately; round trip 22 minutes; 4 cars.

Pier and River: Service interval 17, 16, 17 and 11 minutes repeated; round trip 60 or 61 minutes; 4 cars.

Late evening services as above (10-20-40-60 pattern).

Sundays

Buckland and Maxton as above (winter 1920/21).

Pier and River: Dep. Pier for River 12 noon, 1 p.m. 2 p.m. thence every 20 minutes as late evening service.

Note: These summer and winter services continued virtually unchanged until 1930 when the "winter" services were dropped and the "summer" services operated all the year round.

Special and additional workings

Football matches, Cricket Week, Shopping Week, Christmas Week, Regatta, etc. One or more extras Buckland and Worthington St. or Sea Front.

Summer Sunday afternoons and evenings: Band performance cars, Sea Front to Buckland. Additional car Buckland and River if required.

Workmen's: Extra at 5.30 p.m. from Pier to Buckland; other service cars also so designated (Monday to Friday and about noon on Saturday.

Sunday School treat specials, Buckland to Worthington St. or as required.

Additional Sunday morning cars: Dep. Buckland for Pier and Maxton for *Buckland*, 9.30; dep. Buckland for Maxton 9.50.

Sunday morning River service (last few years only); dep. River 10.30 and 11.30.

Timetable

For many years a red folder pocket timetable was issued to the public.

Power Supply and Current Collection

Dover Corporation did not originally supply its own electrical power for the tramways but purchased it from the Dover Electricity Supply Company, which it took over in 1904. For the opening of the tramways, the company supplemented the equipment in their Park Street Power Station to meet the extra demand. The additional plant installed in 1895 comprised two Babcock & Wilcox water tube boilers, two horizontal tandem compound McIntosh & Seymour engines and four Brush alternators, driving dynamos at 100 K.W.H. This equipment was coupled to four-pole Thomson-Houston generators.

The current was fed to the overhead wires through feeder pillars at first only at the Worthington St. Junction, but later at the usual half mile intervals. There were originally centre posts in the Market Place, King Street and Biggin Street and side bracket suspension for the rest. Fluted cast-iron bases, scroll-work and ball & spike finials of the design common at the time were used. Some of the centre posts had street lamps mounted on top of them, but these were of a heavy and not particularly attractive design. The overhead wiring was laid out for the "Side Running" system common in the early days. Thus, the side brackets were very short and nearly all the side posts were mounted on the south side of the road. The trolley masts on the cars were correspondingly well offset to one side of the upper deck and they had to be placed on the track so that this was the south side. Nevertheless, the trolley poles had to reach well out to the side on the outer cars at passing loops. (This was likened by G. L. Gundry to a "Boarding house reach"). Of necessity the cars had swivel trolley heads. The wires were rigidly attached by insulators to the bracket posts.

Although in later years, the rigid suspension was replaced by flexible bowstrings, the short bracket arms and side running were retained and did present difficulties when some covered top cars were obtained. The open-top West Hartlepool cars had the trolley mast well offset to one side, but they stood lower than the earlier cars and when on the outer track of a loop, their poles could foul the roof of a covered car on the inner track and consequently several bracket arms had to be lengthened, and the wires brought nearer to the track centre-line.

As an additional safeguard, all covered top cars were fitted with a simple travelling device. A metal rod was fixed below the upper part of the trolley pole and had a kink at each end. The trolley rope was threaded through a ring which ran on the rod, taking the rope with it. When the trolley was being turned at the terminus, the ring was flicked into the upper kink and the rope hung from near the trolleyhead

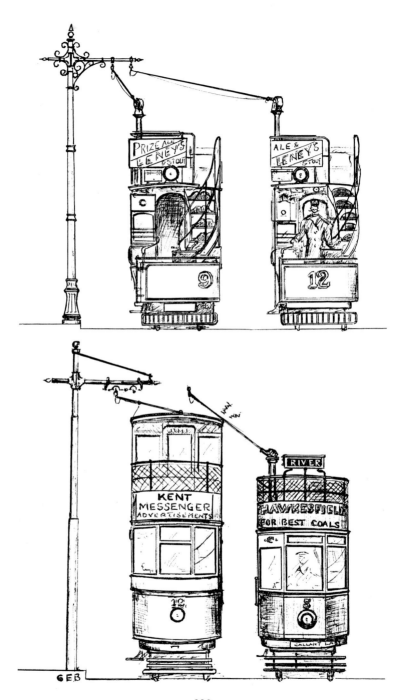

in the usual way, but once the head was on the wire, the ring was flicked down into the lower kink so that the rope hung close to the side of the car and the free end was secured in a cleat on the corner pillar of the upper deck.

Financial Notes

Sound financial judgement and advice is just as important as technical knowledge and expertise in the planning of a business. The Dover tramway undertaking certainly had the latter but it is difficult to be as certain about the former if the aim was to provide a viable service. At the commencement of the tram service the fares were much less than those charged by the horse-bus operators and it is now impossible to know whether all the passengers carried in those early years would have been prepared to pay a slightly higher price for each journey. During the first six years the excess of receipts over operating expenses was about £3,000 per annum. From this sum debt charges had to be paid on the loan raised to meet the initial outlay on cars, track and equipment. Any balance was used in aid of the general rate and no attempt was made to set aside sums in a renewals fund to make provision for future replacements.

Within ten years operating costs exceeded receipts although income from fares had risen from £8,977 in the year 1898-99 to £11,057 in the year 1907-8. During the same period wages paid had increased from £2,338 to £3,719, electrical current supplied from £2,245 to £4,790 and repairs from £350 to £2,441 per annum. The opening of the River service added further debt charges but made little impact on the revenues of the undertaking. It is now difficult to appreciate the reasons for the low initial fares or the failure to set aside sums for renewing and replacing cars, track and equipment. Other factors, however, contributed to the deficits, one such item being the high cost of electricity supplied to the tramway undertaking.

For some unknown reason, since the Corporation operated its own electricity undertaking from 1904 onwards, the cost of power for the trams was always high in comparison with that paid by other undertakings in Kent. The cost of current per B.O.T. unit varied between $2\frac{1}{2}$d. and $2\frac{3}{4}$d. from 1912 to 1919; it increased to 3d. in the following year and to 4d. from 1921 to 1923 inclusive. In 1924 it was reduced to $2\frac{1}{4}$d. and then the price gradually decreased each ear being 1.874d. in 1925 and 1.3d. in the final year of operation 1936. It was surprising that no approach was made by the Tramway Committee to the Electricity Committee about a reduced charge until November, 1931. Indeed it is doubtful if this request would ever have been made but for the fact that the Traffic Commissioners for the South Eastern Area, sitting at Margate, drew the Corporation's attention to the high

---

167. Side running trolleys in theory and practice!

Sketch by G. E. Baddeley.

charge for each unit of current supplied to the tramway undertaking.

From the year 1907-8 to 1928-9 rate aid was necessary in order to keep the tramway operating and in the year 1921-22 the contribution almost reached £9,000. Fare increases were introduced during the early years of the first world war and a 50 per cent increase was imposesd in 1919. The receipts from fares rose from £12,737 in the year 1911-12 to £15,646 in 1915-16 and to £19,832 in 1919-20. In February, 1923 when the fares were reduced, the receipts remained steady and continued at about the 1919-20 level until the final year of operation. On the other hand traffic expenses (consisting mainly of wages) increased from £3,497 in the year 1911-12 to £8,983 in 1920-21, severe increases taking place in 1915, 1919 and 1920. During the period when the undertaking was receiving rate aid, small contributions were made to a renewals fund but in order to prevent the situation which arose after the first world war, when repair costs were in the region of £10,000 per annum, it would have been necessary to contribute sums on a replacement cost basis from the first year of operation. The situation improved year by year after 1923 when the cost of electricity began to fall and the backlog of repairs, due to the lack of maintenance in the war years, had been overcome.

The undertaking was, however, not in a position to purchase new cars to replace its existing ageing stock nor was the management able to speed up the service due to the fact that the track was basically at single line with passing loops. The Manager made some excellent purchases of second-hand cars at bargain prices from other undertakings to keep the service in operation and without these it is doubtful whether it would have continued until December, 1936 unless substantial rate aid had been forthcoming. In an attempt to reduce costs in March, 1933 the Tramway Committee debated a report from the Manager in connection with the possible acceleration of the service. In this report the Manager gave his views as to the reasons for the average speed of the cars being only 6.15 miles per hour and these included, too many stopping places, obstruction caused by other traffic and the breaking of the through service from Pier to Buckland due to road and track repairs. All these factors contributed to difficulties encountered by a management attempting to reduce costs and increase the revenue per car mile.

From 1925 onwards the tramway undertaking accounts again showed an operating or revenue surplus but rate aid was still required to meet part of the debt charges until 1929. The situation improved as the initial and early loans which had been raised for periods of fifteen, twenty and thirty years were repaid and the cost of second-hand cars was met from revenue or renewals fund. When it became apparent that agreement was about to be reached with the East Kent Road Car Company for the provision of bus services to replace the tramway, only essential repair work was authorised by the Tramway Committee. It was therefore possible in the period 1934-36 to build up sufficient reserves to repay all the outstanding loans and provide for reinstatement works when the undertaking ceased to exist on the 31st December, 1936.

FARES

From the opening in 1897, a universal fare of one penny was charged. As the Maxton cars only ran to Worthington Street, a transfer ticket, still at one penny, was issued between The Pier and Maxton.

In 1900 ½d. single fares were introduced on early cars until 8.30 a.m., and the cars on which this facility was available were labelled "½d.".

When the extension to River opened on 2nd October 1905, a penny fare was introduced between Buckland and River, the throughout fare from River to the Pier being 2d.

Schoolchildren's return tickets at one penny for the return journey were introduced during school hours in the latter half of 1910.

After this, there were no alterations to the fare scale until late in 1917, when a fare increase was made necessary by the circumstances of the war. This scale was introduced just after the serious accident mentioned elsewhere, which was a most unfortunate time, and the increase met with some resistance on the part of the public.

The universal penny fare was replaced by the following penny stages:— Worthington Street—Buckland; Worthington Street—Pier; Worthington Street—Maxton and Buckland—River. Penny overlap stages were introduced from Tower Hamlets across the Worthington Street stage to New Bridge on the main line, and by transfer to Priory Station on the Maxton Line.

The schoolchildren's penny return fare was withdrawn, but workmen's penny fares from Buckland to Maxton and the Pier were retained. Presumably, the fare from Pier to Buckland and River was increased to 2d. and 3d. respectively.

A further increase was introduced in the 1919/20 period when the minimum fare became 1½d., and the following fares were brought into operation:—

1½d. Fares: Pier to Worthington Street.
New Bridge to "The Engineer", Folkestone Road (transfer).
New Bridge to Tower Hamlets.
Worthington Street to Maxton.
"The Engineer" to Tower Hamlets (transfer).
Worthington Street to Buckland.
Cherry Tree Avenue to "Cricketers Inn", Lower Road.
Buckland to River.

2d. Fares:	Pier to "The Engineer", Folkestone Road (Transfer).
	Pier to Tower Hamlets.
	New Bridge to Cherry Tree Avenue.
	"The Engineer" to Cherry Tree Avenue (Transfer).
	Tower Hamlets to "The Cricketers" Inn.
3d. Fares:	Pier to Buckland.
	New Bridge to "The Cricketers" Inn.
	Worthington Street to River.
4d. Fares:	Pier to River.

The penny workmen's fare between Pier and Buckland was retained, but there were many inconsistencies in this fare table, some of which were corrected in subsequent fare revisions.

In December 1920, the twopenny fare from New Bridge to Cherry Tree Avenue was extended to Buckland, followed in the early part of 1921 by a new twopenny fare from Worthington Street to the top of Crabble Hill, which was introduced to help engender traffic to and from the new Kearsney Housing Estate.

A new facility introduced in the late summer of 1921 was a $1\frac{1}{2}$d. Children's return fare over any adult $1\frac{1}{2}$d. stage. This ticket was also available as a child single fare over any two adult stages. At the same time a new threepenny adult transfer fare was introduced between Buckland and Maxton.

A fare reduction took place early in 1923, when a new minimum penny fare was introduced for stages ten minutes in length, except between Buckland and River, which remained at $1\frac{1}{2}$d., together with a $1\frac{1}{2}$d. stage between Worthington Street and Crabble Hill. The two penny overlap between Buckland and New Bridge (amongst others) disappeared with this farescale.

In the early part of 1924 a new twopenny stage appeared from New Bridge to the Top of Crabble Hill, whilst, later in the same year, a $1\frac{1}{2}$d. farestage was introduced between New Bridge and Buckland direct, or Maxton by transfer at Worthington Street.

In the summer of 1925, overlap fares presumably $1\frac{1}{2}$d. (Adult) were introduced as follows:— Pier and Tower Hamlets; Pier and "The Engineer", Folkestone Road; Maxton and Tower Hamlets and "The Engineer" to Buckland, some of these being transfer fares. At the same time the fare between River and Tower Hamlets became 2d.

Books of prepaid discount tickets were offered for sale in 1927. These were made up in books of 24 one penny or three-halfpenny tickets. They were sold to the public at 1/10 and 2/9 respectively, but were not a success, as interested purchasers had to go to the Tramway Offices to get them, in consequence of which they were soon withdrawn.

Further fare reductions took place in 1929 (June) when the $1\frac{1}{2}$d. stage between the "Cricketers" and Cherry Tree Avenue was extended to Beaconsfield Road; the 2d. stage from River to Tower Hamlets was extended to Worthington Street, whilst a new 2½d. fare appeared from River to New Bridge (direct). A 2½d. transfer fare was also introduced between River and "The Engineer", Folkestone Road.

At the end of 1929 the 1½d. minimum fare between River and Buckland was reduced to one penny and a new 1½d. stage appeared from River to Cherry Tree Avenue (later extended to Beaconsfield Road).

The last fare alteration before the tramways were withdrawn in 1936, was the introduction of a new penny stage from Beaconsfield Road to the top of Crabble Hill on 30th April 1934.

TICKETS

From the opening of the system until 1919 tickets were supplied in perforated rolls and were printed with full geographical stages as follows:— "Pier to Worthington Street"; "Worthington Street— Maxton" etc. They were cancelled by hand clippers, instead of the more usual Bell Punch. Persons making the full journey between the Pier and Buckland or Maxton had their tickets clipped twice, which led to some confusion, particularly with the Maxton transfers. A similar ticket issuing system was used at Norwich.

Although a twopenny fare was introduced on the extension of the tramways to River in 1905, no specimens have been seen, but it is presumed they were of the same style as the penny tickets described above, the only difference being in the colour. (Specimens seen of these 1d. tickets were usually white, (one was violet), with black printing and red overprint numbers or letters probably to indicate the day of the week.)

The Bell Punch system of cancellation was brought into use with the fare increase of 1920. As quoted in the section dealing with fares, the fare range was from 1½d. to 4d., which called for tickets in various colours. The scheme introduced was 1½d. White; 2d. Blue; 3d. pink and 4d. green.

When the children's 1½d. return fare was brought into operation twelve months later, the tickets used were coloured yellow, with red overprints.

The 1927 discount tickets were coloured orange and were printed with farestage names in the same style as the ordinary single tickets.

When the 1½d. Child's return tickets were withdrawn in November 1930, they were replaced with a ½d. Child single fare, the ticket for which was coloured buff, and covered any penny adult stage. It was issued to children between the ages of 4 and 14, also students in possession of the appropriate certificate.

From then until the close of the system, there were sundry adjustments to the fares which affected the printed matter, the colours became 1d. white, 1½d. blue, 2d. salmon, 2½d. orange & 3d. green.

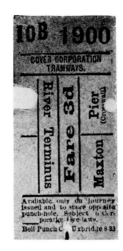
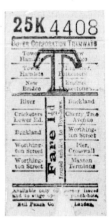

168. Dover Corporation tram tickets, from the Omnibus Society's collection. The early tickets were perforated top and bottom, but unfortunately this does not show in the photograph.

Photographed by A. D. Packer.

There was also a square half size 1d. prepaid ticket with numbered stages coloured cerise.

With the final style there was a long white ticket divided in two with two horizontal rules. The upper half read ADULT Fare 1d. (upwards) and the lower half CHILD Fare 1d. (also reading upwards) in the centre with named stages on either side.

DOVER CORPORATION TRAMWAYS — FINAL FLEET LIST.

ber	Type	Origin	Colour
1.	Open top 4 window, vestibuled.	ex-West Hartlepool.	Dark red and ivory.
2.	,, ,, ,, ,, ,,	,, ,,	Green and ivory.
5.	,, ,, ,, ,, ,,	,,	Dark red and ivory.
7.	Covered top 4 window. ,,	ex-Birmingham & Midland.	,, ,, ,, ,,
9.	Covered top 3 window vestibuled.	ex.Darlington.	Dark red and ivory (formerly green & ivory)
0.	Covered top 4 window.	ex-Birmingham & Midland.	Dark red and ivory.
2.	Covered top 4 window vestibuled.		Green and cream.
3.	Open top 5 window, vestibuled.	Original stock rebuilt.	Green and ivory.
4.	Covered top 4 window.	ex-Birmingham & Midland.	Dark red and ivory.
5.	Open top 5 window.	Original stock rebuilt.	Green and ivory.
6.	Open top 5 window vestibuled.		
7.	Covered top 4 window.	ex-Birmingham & Midland.	Dark red and ivory.
8.	—	Scrapped and not replaced.	—
1.	Covered top 3 window vestibuled.	ex-Birmingham Corporation.	Dark Blue & cream.
2.	Open top 3 window vestibuled.	,, ,,	Green and ivory.
4.	Open top 3 window.	Original stock.	Dark red and ivory.
7.	Covered top 3 window.	(ex-B & M top covers)	(formerly green & ivory).

TE — All Dover cars were on single trucks of Brill type.
Nos. 13, 15, 16, 23 and 24, were latterly spare cars and little used.
Only open top cars were permitted to run to River, usually Nos. 1–5 and 22.

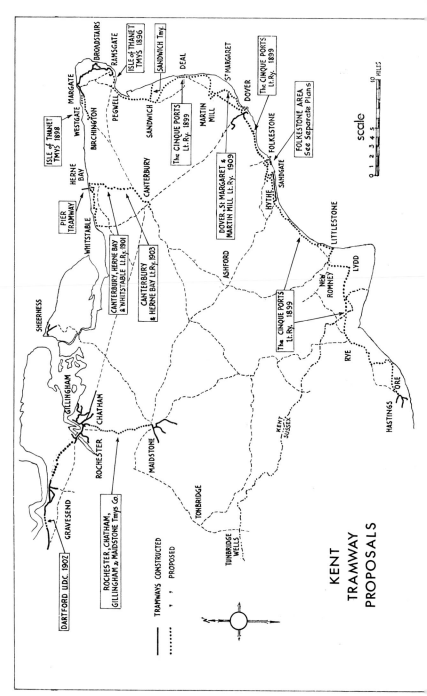

KENT
TRAMWAY
PROPOSALS

TRAMWAYS CONSTRUCTED
" " " PROPOSED

scale
0 1 2 3 4 5   10
                                   MILES

DARTFORD U.D.C. 1902

ROCHESTER, CHATHAM,
GILLINGHAM & MAIDSTONE Tmys Co.

ISLE of THANET TMYS 1898

PIER TRAMWAY

CANTERBURY, HERNE BAY
& WHITSTABLE Lt.Ry. 1901

CANTERBURY
& HERNE BAY Lt.Ry. 1903

ISLE of THANET
TMYS 1896

SANDWICH Tmy.

The CINQUE PORTS
Lt.Ry. 1899

DOVER, St MARGARET &
MARTIN MILL Lt.Ry. 1909

The CINQUE PORTS
Lt.Ry. 1899

FOLKESTONE AREA
See Separate Plans

The CINQUE PORTS
Lt.Ry. 1899

SHEERNESS
GILLINGHAM
CHATHAM
ROCHESTER
GRAVESEND
MAIDSTONE
WHITSTABLE
HERNE BAY
BIRCHINGTON
WESTGATE
MARGATE
BROADSTAIRS
RAMSGATE
PEGWELL
CANTERBURY
SANDWICH
DEAL
ST MARGARET
MARTIN MILL
DOVER
FOLKESTONE
SANDGATE
HYTHE
ASHFORD
LITTLESTONE
LYDD
NEW ROMNEY
RYE
ORE
HASTINGS
TONBRIDGE
TUNBRIDGE WELLS
KENT
SUSSEX

338

CHAPTER EIGHT

PROPOSED TRAMWAYS IN KENT

THE object of this chapter is not so much to deal with the various projected extensions to existing tramways which did not materialize, as these formed part of the story of those undertakings and were more properly described in the chapters devoted to them. In this chapter we are more concerned with those complete systems which were proposed and in some cases authorized, but were never constructed.

Some of these were to have been on a most gradiose scale, quite beyond the traffic potential of the day and it leads one to wonder how potential traffic was measured in those far off days. We hear nothing of the refined techniques used by present day traffic experts to evaluate the relative advantages of several alternative routes offered; the decision was sometimes made by the Transport Committee of the local authority or the Company's Board of Directors, but more often it was left to the Consulting Engineer, who though he may have been well equipped to weigh up the technical advantages and hazards of one route as compared with another, i.e. steep hills, sharp corners, low bridges etc., he probably had no specialized training in the measurement of passenger potential and had to rely on his instinct or counting chimney pots to guess how many people would use the route when opened. Even the Manager when appointed was often styled "General Manager and Engineer" with emphasis on his engineering qualifications; and indeed another generation was to pass before one could obtain qualifications in Traffic Management.

Now to deal with the specific proposals:—

1. *Horns Cross — Craylands.*

Although this was a proposal sponsored by an undertaking which did operate subsequently, this line merits mention here as it would have linked a system described in Volume 1 of this book, with a system described in another work. Although it is probably the shortest line to be dealt with in this chapter, it might well have been the most important, had it materialized. Only one and a half miles in length it would have linked the Gravesend-Northfleet system with Dartford and thence with Bexley, Woolwich and London. The proposal was put up by the Dartford U.D.C. in 1902 and strongly supported by the Gravesend and Bexley undertakings as well as the Balfour, Beatty Group who constructed both the Bexley and Dartford systems and worked the latter until 1917. In fact the Gravesend tramways were converted to standard gauge on electrification, largely with this link-up

169. Opposite—Map of proposed tramway routes in Kent, which never materialized.   E. Beddard.

170. The bus with which the Gravesend Tramways inaugurated the bus service between Horns Cross and the "George & Dragon", Swanscombe. Unknown source.

in mind. On the other hand, it was always strenuously opposed by the railway company, who could see it as undermining their traffic. The Bill eventually received Royal Assent in 1912, but by this time it was too late as the Gravesend Company, tired of waiting, had put on a motor-bus service from Gravesend to Dartford, which competed directly with the Dartford-Horns Cross tram service.

2. *Rochester, Chatham, Gravesend and Maidstone Tramways Co.*

Much has already been said about this abortive undertaking in Chapter 2, Vol. 1 and it suffices to say here that had it materialized, the major towns of West Kent would have been linked with each other by tramway. If the Horns Cross—Craylands line had also been built there would have been a direct link with London and Gravesend would have been the meeting place of extensive networks on two gauges. The whole complex would have become a serious competitor with the main line railways.

Chapter 2. (Vol. 1) describes how, when the Company's Bill was withdrawn, the Chatham Company and Rochester Corporation stepped in and took over some of the powers, but although some lines were constructed, they were only a drop in the ocean compared with the whole scheme.

3. *Canterbury, Herne Bay & Whitstable Light Railway Co.*

This company obtained powers in 1901, under the Light Railways Act of 1896, to construct a line some 16 miles long, from Canterbury East Station, along the Stour Valley to Sturry, Calcott Hill, Herne

Common, Herne Street, Eddington and Herne Bay, whence it would have run westward along the coast to Hampton, Swalecliffe, Tankerton and Whitstable. It was to have been an electric street tramway with overhead wires supported by posts of "ornamental design" and the cars were to have been luxuriously appointed, able to run as open cars in the summer and as closed cars in the winter. Additional short workings and workmen's cars would have been operated as necessary. The journey would have taken about two hours and the fare would have been one shilling and four pence. The power station was to have been at the bottom of the hill at Sturry: there was also to have been a loop line in Herne Bay, passing the station and the track gauge was to have been 3 feet 6 inches.

It is said that the Kent County Council, the Herne Bay U.D.C. and Whitstable U.D.C. viewed the proposals with favour, but the Canterbury authorities did not, because of the very narrow streets in the city; nor did the London, Chatham and Dover Railway Company and consequently the project was stifled.

Another similar scheme, "The Canterbury & Herne Bay Light Railway Company" was authorized to construct $9\frac{1}{2}$ miles of route also on the 3 ft. 6 in. gauge in 1903, but this also came to nothing.

4. *Various Tramway Proposals in the Folkestone Area*

These proposals overlapped to some extent and it has, therefore, been found expedient to group them together under one heading, although they were put forward in succession by several different interests. The B.T-H. prepared a Folkestone scheme in 1897 through a subsidiary, the "Folkestone & District Electric Railway Co." and soon afterward in 1898 the B.E.T. launched a similar scheme under the title "Sandgate & Hythe Electric Co." This was clearly connected with their plan to take over the Sandgate horse tramway, but direct access to Folkestone was the stumbling block, being barred by the Leas, a select area with its private roads, toll gates and steep gradients; hence the tramway would have had to take a roundabout inland route via Cheriton to connect Sandgate with Folkestone.

Soon after the above failed to materialize, in November 1900, the "Sandgate, Cheriton and Folkestone Light Railways" applied for permission to construct the following lines, which would have been of standard gauge, so as to connect with the horse tramway near its eastern end:—

Railway No. 1. — Length — 0 miles, 4 furlongs, 4.00 chains.
From Folkestone Borough boundary in Upper Folkestone Road, down Sandgate Hill and in Sandgate High Street to the Corner of Military Road.

Railway No. 2. — Length — 1 mile, 0 furlongs, 3.50 chains.
Along Military Road for 300 yards, then on

	private right of way across country to the south end of Risborough Lane.
Railway No. 3.	— Length — 0 miles, 2 furlongs, 6.70 chains. Along Risborough Lane and Cheriton Street to Folkestone Borough boundary.
Railway No. 4.	— Length — 2 miles, 0 furlongs, 8.30 chains. From Folkestone Borough boundary, along Cheriton Road, Radnor Park Road, Sussex Road, Bradstone Avenue, Bradstone Road, Tontine Street and Harbour Street to the Inner Harbour.
Railway No. 5.	— Length — 0 miles, 5 furlongs, 0.60 chains. Along Cheriton Street, from Stanley Road to Horn Street.
Railway No. 5A.	— Length — 0 miles, 0 furlongs, 2.00 chains. South-west curve at the junction of Cheriton Street and Risborough Lane.

This proposal amounted to a total of 4 miles, 5 furlongs and 5.10 chains, but was not followed up.

The local authorities, namely Folkestone Corporation and Cheriton Urban District Council, countered by launching their own tramway schemes, this time to be laid to the 3 ft. 6 in. gauge. Folkestone Corporation introduced a Bill in the 1901 Session of Parliament for 2 miles, 5 furlongs 8.73 chains of tramway, made up as follows: —

Tramway No. 1.	— Length — 1 mile, 0 furlongs, 8.73 chains. From the Cheriton U.D.C. boundary along Cheriton Road to Folkestone Central Station.
Tramway No. 2.	— Length — 1 mile, 0 furlongs, 2.00 chains. From Folkestone Central Station, via Park Road and Tontine Street to the Inner Harbour.
Tramway No. 3.	— Length — 0 miles, 4 furlongs, 7.12 chains. From Folkestone Central Station via Cheriton Road to the Town Hall.

Of these tramways, Nos. 1 & 2 were authorized, except for a passing loop by the Pavilion. Meanwhile, at the same time Cheriton U.D.C. applied for a complementary scheme, comprising 1 mile, 4 furlongs, 3.95 chains of tramway, connecting with the Folkestone system at the boundary in Cheriton Road. These were defined as follows:—

Tramway No. 1.	— Length 0 miles, 4 furlongs, 7.5 chains. From the boundary with Hythe, along Horn Street to Cheriton Street.
Tramway No. 2.	— Length — 0 miles, 4 furlongs, 9.5 chains. A continuation along Cheriton Street from Horn Street to Stanley Road. (This section would have had a maximum gradient of 1 in 11.3).
Tramway No. 3.	— Length — 0 miles, 4 furlongs, 9.5 chains.

In Risborough Lane from Cheriton Street to
the Railway bridge.

Tramway No. 4. — Length — 0 miles, 1 furlong, 7.45 chains.
Along Cheriton Street from Stanley Road to
the Folkestone Borough boundary, to join
Folkestone Tramway No. 1.

These powers were granted but nothing was done to implement
them. However, in 1904, Folkestone Corporation re-applied for their
Tramway No. 3 which had been rejected in their 1901 scheme and
applied for two additional lines as follows:—

Tramway No. 4. — Length — 0 miles, 1 furlong, 5.18 chains.
From the Town Hall via Rendezvous Street to
Tontine Street.
This line would have had a maximum gradient
of 1 in 10.12.

Tramway No. 5. — Length — 0 mlies, 3 furlongs, 8.94 chains.
From Harbour Street via Lower Sandgate Road
and Marine Terrace to Victoria Pier.

A Provisional Order was granted for the above.

No depot is mentioned for either scheme and it can be assumed
that the lines, if built would have been leased to a company to
operate. Conduit tramways in Paris & Bournemouth were visited in
1903.

The Provisional Order contained an undertaking insisted on by the
Earl of Radnor, who owned much of the land in the area, not to
adopt the overhead trolley system of current collection and subsequently when difficulties were encountered, his Lordship refused
to waive his objection. Consequently, the Corporation looked into
the possibility of installing the side conduit system as used on part
of the Bournemouth tramways with a slot in one of the running rails.
A contract for the construction of the Folkestone Corporation
Tramways was awarded to W. Griffiths & Co., but was withdrawn
early in April 1905 when the Council decided by 9 votes to 8 not to
proceed further with the scheme. At that time, no more than some
minor preliminary road works had been undertaken. On 5th May
it was announced that the extension of time allowed under the
Folkestone Tramways Act was about to lapse and no moves were
taken to extend it further. (A rival scheme in 1901 was the Sandgate,
Cheriton & Folkestone Light Railway Co., whose application for $4\frac{3}{4}$
miles was thrown out.)

In the circumstances, the Corporation raised no objection to
private enterprise stepping in and two schemes were put forward in
1906 one of which submitted by the Traction & Power Securities Ltd.
proved unacceptable because it depended on the use of overhead
wires. The other scheme was put up by the National Electric

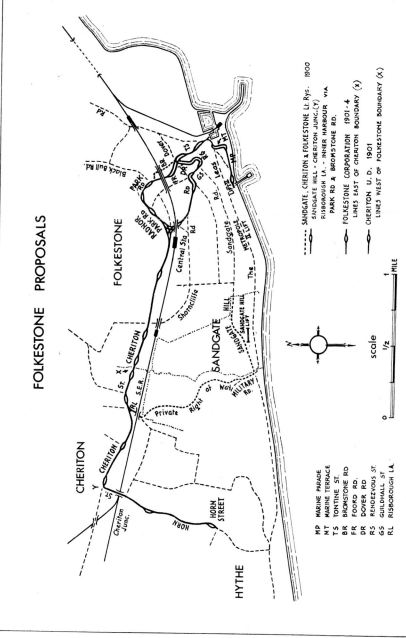

FOLKESTONE PROPOSALS

CHERITON

FOLKESTONE

SANDGATE

HYTHE

HORN STREET

Cheriton Junc.

Central Sta.

Shorncliffe

Sandgate Hill

MILITARY RD.

Right of Way

Private

SANDGATE HILL LIFT

METROPOLE LIFT

The Leas

MP MARINE PARADE
MT MARINE TERRACE
TS TONTINE ST.
BR BROMSTONE RD
FR FOORD RD.
DR DOVER RD
RS RENDEZVOUS ST.
GS GUILDHALL ST.
RL RISBOROUGH LA.

----- SANDGATE, CHERITON & FOLKESTONE Lt. Rys. 1900
──○── SANDGATE HILL - CHERITON JUNC. (Y)
RISBOROUGH LA. - INNER HARBOUR VIA PARK RD & BROMSTONE RD.
FOLKESTONE CORPORATION 1901-4
──●── LINES EAST OF CHERITON BOUNDARY (X)
CHERITON U.D. 1901
──○── LINES WEST OF FOLKESTONE BOUNDARY (X)

scale

N

0   ½   1 MILE

construction Co. (no connection with the short lived company with a similar title mentioned in Chapter 1. Vol.1) The N.E.C.* obtained their own Light Railway Order in 1906 for a system 13 miles long (including the lines proposed by the Corporation, whose powers were to be taken over), also including the Sandgate-Hythe horse tramway, which they hoped to take over. All these lines were to be equipped on the "Dolter" Surface Contact System and to be operated by a subsidiary company known as the "Folkestone, Sandgate & Hythe Tramways Company". The Dolter system depended on powerful magnets suspended under each car, which attracted and energized mechanical switches fixed to the underside of studs set at intervals in the roadway between the running rails. It was already in use on the Bois de Boulogne line in Paris and at the time the N.E.C. had tramways using the Dolter system under construction at Mexborough in Yorkshire and at Torquay in Devon.

On 10th October 1906, a party of Folkestone Councillors visited Yorkshire and were taken for a demonstration run on the newly opened first section of the Mexborough & Swinton tramway. All went according to plan and they came away well satisfied. Thus had the N.E.C. been ready to start work at once at Folkestone, Great Britain might well have had another tramway undertaking, one which was worked on the Dolter Surface Contact System. One can even envisage the cars running, since the N.E.C. acquired standard Brush three window cars mounted on Mountain & Gibson radial trucks for both Mexborough and Torquay and there is no reason to suppose that those at Folkestone would have been different. However, by the time they were ready to start work at Folkestone, the defects of the Dolter system had begun to manifest themselves to an alarming extent at Mexborough and to a lesser degree at Torquay; the switches under the studs in the road which were supposed to make them alive only when a car was passing over them, sometimes failed to operate necessitating the car coasting over them, or worse still, they occasionally remained alive after the car had passed, with possible dire consequences to horses or pedestrians who were foolish enough to step on them, so that elaborate precautions had to be taken and minor electrical leakage was fairly common. The Dolter system was the first of the three stud systems tried in Great Britain and was the worst offender in this respect. In consequence, the N.E.C. had to look again at those proposals for tramway systems still on their books and withdrew those which depended on the absence of overhead

---

171. Opposite—Map of proposed tramways in Folkestone.

E. Beddard after V. Goldberg.

---

*The N.E.C. owned tramways at Torquay, Rhondda, Oxford (horse), Mexborough, Ossett & Musselburgh.

172. A Tilling-Stevens single decker of the Folkestone District Road Car Co. on the Folkestone-Hythe service.　　　Courtesy N. N. Forbes.

wires, namely Oxford and Folkestone. In any case, the Chairman of the Parliamentary Committee which sat in 1909, objected to the stud system because of its inherent danger and considered the slot conduit system too costly for all but the largest and busiest undertakings.

In view of the difficulties at Folkestone, the Sandgate U.D.C., withdrew the notice given on 27th January 1906, that it intended to acquire so much of the Sandgate and Hythe horse tramway as lay within its area.

In the meantime, motor-vehicle operators stepped in and even in March 1905, a bus service had been started from Dover to Lydd, passing through Folkestone.

5.　*Tramway at Sandwich.*

In 1895, there was a proposal to construct a $2\frac{1}{2}$ mile tramway to run from Sandwich Town to the beach. Possibly this might have been of similar type to the Rye & Camber line in Sussex (a narrow gauge steam railway), or perhaps a proper tramway. No plan was deposited nor application made for a Bill in Parliament.

6.　*Tramways right round the coast.*

Mention has already been made in Chapter 5, of the 1871 proposal for the "Dover, Deal, Sandwich and Ramsgate Tramway", which was to have been 21 miles, 24 chains long. The Bill was rejected and similar proposals came up in the following year under the title "Kent Tramways Co." sponsored by J. V. Dick, this was to be 29 miles 48 chains. An Act was passed in 1873, but no work was done and the £3,750 deposit forfeited! However, in November 1899, similar proposals were put forward under the title "Cinque Ports Light Railway Co." for the construction of a light railway of tramway type to connect the Thanet Company's line (shortly to be opened) with Hastings via Dover Corporation Tramways, meeting them at the Market Square and running over Dover tracks as far as Maxton, whence its own tracks would be resumed along the Dover-Folkestone Road, through Folkestone and Sandgate (presumably over the proposed Folkestone Tramways and the existing Sandgate-Hythe horse tramway) and on round the coast into Sussex, finishing at Hastings. This lengthy 68 mile line of 3 ft. 6 in. gauge would have been laid mainly with single track and passing loops and the current was to be taken from overhead wires. It is presumed that the cars would have been of the then current design, i.e. similar to those already in use at Dover. It was to cost £330,712. The Dover Borough Engineer reported unfavourably on the scheme saying that it would interfere with the working of their own tramway system and the proposal which gained very little support, was soon dropped.

The Thanet Company's proposals for extensions to its system to Birchington, Pegwell Bay etc., have already been mentioned in Chapter 5.

7. *The Dover, St. Margarets and Martin Mill Light Railway.*

Mention has been made of this scheme in Chapter 7. The Dover, St. Margarets and Martin Mill project was the subject of a Light Railway Order in 1909 and was defined as follows:—

Railway No. 1. — Length — 0 miles, 3 furlongs, 7.50 chains.
Wholly situated in the Parish of Dover and commencing in Northampton Street by a junction with the existing Dover Corporation Tramway No. 2 at a point 0.5 chains west of the junction of Northampton Street and New Bridge, passing thence along New Bridge Camden Crescent, Liverpool Street, Douro Place, Marine Parade and East Cliff Road and terminating at the westerly junction of East Cliff Road and East Cliff Back Road.

Railway No. 2. — Length — 2 miles, 7 furlongs, 2.50 chains.
Situated in the Parishes of Dover, Gunston, St. Margaret's at Cliffe (detached), West Cliffe and St. Margaret's at Cliffe, commencing by a junction with Railway No. 1 at its termination, passing thence in a north-easterly direction along East Cliff Road and Athol Terrace, thence on a new road which it was proposed to make on lands belonging or reputed to belong to the War Department and to the Admiralty and to the

	Dover Undercliffe Syndicate, by way of Langdon Hole to the summit of the cliff, over Corn Hill, thence across Wanstone and Reach Court farms and terminating at a point in the Upper Road, 19 chains or thereabouts west of the junction of that road with Sea Street, St. Margaret's.
Railway No. 3.	— Length — 1 mile, 0 furlongs, 9.60 chains. Situated in the Parishes of St. Margaret's at Cliffe, West Cliffe, and East Langdon, commencing by a junction with Railway No. 2 at its termination, passing thence in a north-westerly direction and termination at a point in the Dover and Deal Road, 12 chains or thereabouts south-west of the junction of the Dover and Deal Road, with the road leading from Martin Mill to St. Margaret's.
Railway No. 4.	— Length — 0 miles, 4 furlongs, 8.25 chains. Wholely situated in the Parish of East Langdon, commencing by a junction with Railway No. 3 at its termination and passing thence in a north-westerly direction over lands to be purchased, along and over public roads leading from Martin Mill to St. Margarets and thence into and along the private road leading to the South Eastern & Chatham Railway's station at Martin Mill and south-west of the entrance to the booking office of the said station.

It may be of interest to note that Railway No. 1 and the East Cliff Road part of Railway No. 2, were practically identical with Tramways Nos. 5 & 7 of the Dover Corporation 1896 Order.

The "New Road" part of Railway No. 2 was in fact partly constructed on a ledge cut in the face of the cliff, but any present day explorer should be warned that there are also remains of various military lines in the area, none of which formed part of the Dover, St. Margarets and Martin Mill Light Railway project, for which no work was undertaken other than the above mentioned ledge.

Conclusions

Of all the schemes described in this chapter, only those for the Folkestone area showed any real promise of success. It may seem strange that there were no specific proposals for tramways in the Kent coalfield area, as most coal-mining areas in other parts of the country have managed to attract tramway development; the answer would appear to lie in the relatively late development of mining in Kent. The area was served by the East Kent Light Railway, but this was a full size steam railway in the Colonel Stephens Group and therefore comes outside the scope of this book. Also, the authors have found no evidence of any tramway proposals in the busy Tonbridge/Tunbridge Wells conurbation, although very early and intensive motor-bus development indicates that there was scope for tramways, had the buses not got in first. Deal was also served by buses at an early date.

APPENDIX E

BIBLIOGRAPHY

The following works have been consulted in the preparation of this volume. They are set out in the order of the chapters to which they refer. Please see also Appendix "A" to Volume 1, which contains general references applicable to both volumes.

(a) *General.*

Garcke's Manual of Electrical Undertakings. — Various dates.
"Modern Tramway" for August 1970. "100 Years of the Tramways Act" G. B. Claydon Ll.B.

(b) *Isle of Thanet.*

"Tramway & Railway World" for April & November 1901.
"Tramway Review" No. 3, 1951. "Accidents will happen" (Accident at Ramsgate).
"Bus & Coach" for August 1937. "Rationalization" (East Kent buses replace Thanet and Dover trams).
"Omnibus Magazine" for December 1957. "Tram & Bus services in Ramsgate" B. H. Whintle.
"Isle of Man Tramways" by F. K. Pearson, David & Charles, Newton Abbot, 1970. (Account of a horse car intended for the Isle of Thanet).

(c) *Folkestone, Hythe & Sandgate Tramway.*

"Buses Illustrated" for July 1950. "Folkestone, Hythe & Sandgate Tramway" (and subsequent correspondence).
"Folkestone Herald" Various quotations from Sandgate Council Minutes.
"Railway Magazine" for October 1950. "The Hythe & Sandgate Tramway" by Charles E. Lee.
"Kent Life" for April 1964. "By Toastrack to Sandgate" by Eric Harrison.

Cliff Railways and Lifts.

"Railway Magazine" for August 1951. "Cliff Railways" by P. W. Gentry.
"Cliff Railways" by G. Body and R. L. Eastleigh. London 1964.
"Folkestone Gazette" for 15th April 1964. "The interesting story of Folkestone's Cliff Lifts" by Eric Harrison.
"Kent Life" for July 1965. "Coastal ups and downs" by Eric Harrison.

Herne Bay Pier Tramway.

Proceedings of the Herne Bay Records Society. Various dates.
"Modern Tramway" for April 1968. "Herne Bay Pier — Three Tramways and a Mystery" by A. Winstan Bond.

Ramsgate Tunnel Railway.

"Railway World" for May 1961. "The Ramsgate Tunnel Railway" by H. C. Towers.
"Modern Tramway" for July 1961. "The Ramsgate Tunnel Railway" by J. H. Price.
"Narrow Gauge Railways of Britain" by F. H. Howson, London 1948.

(d) *Dover Corporation Tramways.*

"Folkestone Herald" for 13th March 1897. Delivery of rails.
"Tramway & Railway World" for October 1897, May 1911 and August 1914.
Bus & Coach" for August 1937. "Rationalization" (See Thanet above).

BIBLIOGRAPHY — Dover (Ctd.)

"Tramway Review" No. 11, 1953. "The Light Railways of Darlington" by G. S. Hearse. (Darlington cars sold to Dover).
"The Tramways of the Black Country" by J. S. Webb, Bloxwich, 1954. (2nd Edition 1974). (Black Country Cars sold to Dover).
"The story of Dover Corporation Tramways" by J. V. Horn, London 1955.
Dover Corporation — Various Council Minutes.
(e) *Proposed Tramways.*
"Chatham Observer" for 28th December 1956. "The longest tramway of them all". (Proposed Canterbury, Herne Bay and Whitstable tramway.)
"Tramway & Railway World" — various short references.
"Electric Railway & Tramway Journal" — various short references.
"Passenger Transport" for May 1963. "Folkestone depends on East Kent Road Car Co." by J. C. Gillham.
"Tramway Review" No. 53, Spring 1968. "Tramways in South Yorkshire" by C. C. Hall. (Folkestone delegation visit Mexborough tramway.)
Board of Trade reports on Tramway and Light Railway Bills and Orders.
Copies of Acts and confirmed Orders.

APPENDIX F

LIST OF MANAGERS (ELECTRIC TRAMWAYS)

(a) *Gravesend & Northfleet.*

A. W. Kipping (from horse tramways)	1902 to 1908	
P. N. Gray	1908 ,, 1914	
A. E. Wray	1914 ,, 1915	
J. C. R. Groves	1915 ,, 1918	
J. Dobson	1918 ,, 1919	
P. R. Blake A.M.I.E.E., A.M.Inst.T.	1919 ,, 1929	

(b) *Chatham & District.*

W. Jensen A.M.I.E.E.	1902 ,, 1927
A. J. Bousfield	1927 ,, 1930

(c) *Sheerness & District.*

W. J. Cutbush	1903 ,, 1904
P. A. Yapp	1904 ,, 1905
H. J. Nesbitt	1905 ,, 1906
A. A. Watkins	1906 ,, 1908
G. L. Kirk	1908 ,, 1913
C. W. Durnford	1913 ,, 1914
A. Charlton	1914 ,, 1917

(remained with Electricity Dept.)

(d) *Maidstone Corporation.*

E. E. Hoadley	1904 ,, 1907
F. E. Saunders	1907 ,, 1910
A. T. Lambert	1910 ,, 1930

(remained with buses & trolleybuses to 1936)

(e) *Isle of Thanet.*

A. A. Tylor	1901 ,, 1902
R. Humphries A.M.I.E.E.	1904 ,, 1907 (acting 1903)
J. A. Forde A.M.I.E.E.	1907 ,, 1937

(f) *Dover Corporation.*

E. C. Carden	1897 ,, 1918
E. H. Bond A.M.I.E.E.	1918 ,, 1936

APPENDIX G

SOME FURTHER NOTES ON GRAVESEND, CHATHAM AND SHEERNESS.

By R. H. Hiscock, Chairman of the Gravesend Historical Society, also by J. F. Parke of the Omnibus Society, J. H. Price & S. L. Harris.

1. GRAVESEND & NORTHFLEET.

(a) *Horse Tramways.*

Apparently four separate schemes were put forward before any tramways were actually constructed in Gravesend & Northfleet and details are available in the Gravesend Corporation Archives.

The fare in 1883 was 2d. for any distance. In 1893, the railway timetable mentions that trams were leaving Northfleet at 9.30 a.m. and Gravesend at 10.00 and running every half hour until 2.30 p.m. and then at 20 minute intervals until 6.0 p.m. after which a 15 minute service was maintained until 10.0 p.m. There was a late car at 11.00 p.m. from Gravesend on Mondays to Saturdays. The Sunday service started from Northfleet and Gravesend at 2.30 and 3.0 p.m. respectively.

According to the "Gravesend Reporter" the last horse car is said to have run on Monday night 10th June 1901 and the lower illustration on page 20, Volume 1, is reputed to be this car taken at the depot before departure. During the interim period between the horse trams finishing and the electric tramways opening, Messrs. Smith & Day's Cycle shop obtained a licence to operate two twelve seater cars, but one of them was involved in a fatal accident when children kept running out in front of them to see then stop suddenly and one child was killed. On 5th April 1902, the Tramways Company applied for permission to run horse buses over the tram route until the generating station was ready to supply them with current, but this request was turned down.

(b) *Electric Tramways.*

The current was turned on at the Corporation's Generating Station by Alderman E. C. Paine on 29th July 1902 and a tramcar ran trials from the depot to Swanscombe immediately.

After the complaints by the Board of Trade examiner, the pavement was set back slightly near the bottom of Windmill Street by the Corporation (see page 24). Both the Corporation and the Company paid towards this work and the trams started running on the Windmill Street route on 4th May 1903.

Cars — It appears from a photograph that during the period when No. 1 was used for advertising "Shrimp Brand" it carried a small destination box below the upper deck handrail. Perhaps all of Nos. 1-4 had them in this position at that time. There were Bostwick gates on the platforms.

Car No. 7 (ex-Taunton) had a single seat on each platform. According to R. C. Sambourne, a spare truck may have come to Gravesend with the two Taunton cars.

Management — Mr. J. C. R. Groves left Gravesend on 14th November 1918 to become Manager at Barrow-in-Furness. He was replaced for the next few months by Mr. J. Dobson, who had previously been Manager at Kimberley, South Africa, but in August 1919, he was appointed to Southampton Corporation Tramways and was succeeded at Gravesend by P. R. Blake.

Operation — Although a "points boy" was sometimes employed at the St. James's Church junction, points were normally worked by the driver leaning over the dash and shifting them with a long point iron. When the through working from the High Street to Pelham Arms commenced, in 1927, a drop lever frog was installed on the overhead junction at St. James's Church.

Northfleet Council complained regularly about various aspects of the tramway operation to which they objected, particularly the lack of decoration on the traction posts, their position, material left lying about on the pavements and that the head lamps on the cars were too bright!

Finance — The finances of the company always seemed to be in a bad way. By 1915, the payment on Preference Shares was 39% in arrear and no ordinary dividends had ever been paid. The capital was then written down and most of the preference shares converted to ordinary shares, 2% being paid on these in 1917, 3% in 1918, 1919 and 1920. No dividend was paid at all in 1921 or 1922 according to the Stock Exchange Year Book.

Fares & Tickets. When the ½d. fare went up to ¾d., conductors were issued with packets of pins to give in lieu of change. There was at one time a 1½d. return fare on the Windmill Street route and a 3d. blue ticket was in use at the time of the closure of the tramways and stocks thereof were used up on the replacing buses. Shilling Scholars' passes were valid for one week anywhere on the system.

Motor Buses. John Parke explains that the main reason why only two of the former Tram Company's buses were handed over to London Transport, was because they were of the "Low Bridge" type and at that time the Board had no use for such vehicles, while Maidstone & District was glad to keep them. It was therefore agreed that they should hand over mainly "Titans" of the "High Bridge" type, drawn from other areas if necessary. In fact some of the "Low Bridge" buses had already been transferred away from Gravesend. (D. H. Jeffery states that registration numbers KP 3055-3057 and not KP 3005-3007 were included among those sold to London Transport.)

2. CHATHAM.

Operation — *Mr. S. L. Harris of Chatham remarks that by the* mid-1920s several of the triangular junctions shown on the map in Volume 1, had been replaced by single junctions allowing movement in two directions only. The crossover at the Brook had been moved to Dock Road for the benefit of cars on a shuttle service "Cemetery-Town Hall" (L. W. S. Heath thinks both crossovers existed latterly.) A crossover was added on the Rainham line at Luton Arches.

Cars — The livery of cars was originally a darker green than that in use latterly. After being tried out on the Borstal and Rainham routes, the ex-Maidstone car spent most of its working life at Chatham on the abovementioned "Cemetery-Town Hall" shuttle service. As well as the carpet seats on this car, No. 43 was fully upholstered during Mr. Bousfield's regime, with seating like that on contemporary Maidstone & District buses, but running the length of the car.

Motor Buses — Apparently it was only the chassis of buses intended for Chatham which finished up at Bath. Some of the original bodies, but mounted on other chassis remained at Chatham and Bath got brand new bodies. (The Kent registration numbers would of course remain with the chassis). The Mr. French referred to on page 58 was virtually the founder of the Maidstone & District Company.

3. SHEERNESS.

(a) *Electric Tramways.*

In an article in "Tramway & Railway World" for 9th August 1906, Mr. Hoogwinkel, writing about bow collectors, stated that on systems that used trolley wheels, there had been accidents due to the trolley leaving the overhead wire at a time of emergency so that the car was deprived of electric braking. He also spoke of complaints about "molten grease dripping on defence-less passengers" and he thought this must refer to the obsolete type of bow used on the Isle of Man. It could never happen with the system he had installed at Sheerness.

He also referred to the Sheerness installation as "one of the affili-ated companies of the late "Electrical Power Distribution Co. Ltd." He said some trouble had been experienced at first owing to the cast iron trolley masts on which the bows were mounted, breaking (see page 124) and said they had now been replaced by steel ones as originally specified. These were of the internal spring pattern. The aluminium strips on the contact surfaces of the bows cost 6s. 6d. each and lasted for 5,000 miles. As they incorporated a lubricating groove, the wear and tear on the overhead wire was less than with an ordinary trolley wheel, even on curves where the strain was greatest. (L. W. S. Heath states that there was a turntable on the street outside the depot.)

(b) *Motor Buses.*

J. F. Parke states that Standen bought out the B.E.T. interest in Sheppey Motors in January 1923, but that his firm was taken over by Maidstone & District on 8th January 1930, thereby reverting to the B.E.T. fold. "Enterprise" was taken over on 19th December of the same year, but there had been a working agreement since 1928.

The garage and staff of Folkestone Motors Ltd. with the rear view of an open motor coach, lettered up optimistically for "Route 77, Folkestone, Sandgate and Hythe. Fares and "Licenced to carry 11 persons" are also shown. These are what competed with the Horse tramway.   Courtesy J. H. Price.

Appendix H.

TABLE OF ELECTRIC TRAMCAR DIMENSIONS

ISLE OF THANET — Gauge 3ft. 6in.

Car Numbers	Date Built	Type of car	Seating In	Seating Out	Side windows	Body builder	Truck	Wheel Base	Motors	Type of Controller	Length: Overall	Over Dashes	Over Corner Pillars	Width: Overall	Over Sills	Height: at Pillars	Lower Saloon	Trolley Plank	Notes
1–20	1900	DD.OT	24	29	4	St. Louis	St. Louis No. 8	6 0	B.T-H GE.58	B.T-H B.18	29 4	28 4	17 10	6 6	6 0	6 4	6 4½	9 8¾	(a, b, c, f)
(I) 21–40	1900	DD.OT	30	38	6	St. Louis	St. Louis No. 13 bogies	4 0	B.T-H. GE.58	B.T.-H. B.18	33 4	32 4	21 0	6 6	6 0	6 4	6 4½	9 8¾	(a, b, c, f)
(II) 21–40	1903	DD.OT	24	32	4½	St. Louis	Brush Aa*	6 0	B.T-H. GE.58	B.T.-H. B.18	28 4	27 4	16 0	6 6	6 0	6 4	6 4½	9 8¾	(a, b, c, f, d)
41–50	1901	DD.OT	24	28	4	Milnes	Brill 21.E	6 0	B.T-H. GE.58	B.T.-H. B.18.	27 8	26 8	16 8	6 3	5 10	6 0	6 9	9 9½	(a, e) later (f) or (g)
51–60	1903	DD.OT	24	26	4	B.E.C.	Brill 21.E	6 0	B.T-H GE.58	B.T.-H. B.18	28 2	27 2	16 8	6 6	5 10	6 3	6 9	9 9½	(a, e, g), later (f)
61	?	Works	—	—	—	Own Works?	Brush Aa	6 0	B.T-H. GE.58	B.T-H. B.18	?	?	?	6 ?	—	—	6 9	9 9½	(g)

DOVER CORPORATION — Gauge 3ft. 6in.

(a) Original Fleet.

Car Numbers	Date Built	Type of car	Seating In	Seating Out	Side windows	Body builder	Truck	Wheel Base	Motors	Type of Controller	Length: Overall	Over Dashes	Over Corner Pillars	Width: Overall	Over Sills	Height: at Pillars	Lower Saloon	Trolley Plank	Notes
1–10	1897	DD.OT	20	24	5	Brush	Peckham Cantilever	6 0	American GE.800	GEC K.2	25 8	25 0	15 0	6 6	5 6	6 0	6 9	9 4½	(c, e, l)
11–14	1898	DD.OT	20	24	5	Milnes	Peckham Cantilever	6 0	Walker 33.N	Walker S.7	25 0	24 0	15 0	6 3	5 6	6 0	6 9	9 4½	(c, e, h)
15–16	1898	DD.OT	20	24	5	Brill	Brill 21.E	6 0	Walker 33.N	Walker S.7	27 0	26 0	16 0	6 3	5 6	6 1½	6 9	9 4½	(c, b, h)
17	1902	DD.OT	22	26	3	ER & TCW.	Brill 21.E	6 0	Dick Kerr 33.N	D.K. S.7	27 6	26 6	16 0	6 3	5 6	6 0	6 7	9 4½	(a, b)
18–21	1905	DD.OT	22	26	3	U.E.C.	Brill 21.E	6 0	Dick Kerr 33.N	D.K. S.7	27 6	26 6	16 0	6 3	5 6	6 0	6 7	9 4½	(b)
22–24	1912	DD.OT	22	26	3	Brush	Brill 21.E	6 6	B.T-H. S.7	GEC- K.10	28 0	27 0	16 0	6 6	5 6	6 0	6 7	9 4½	(e)
25–27	1920	DD.OT	22	26	3	E.E.	E.E. "Preston"	7 6	E.E. DK. 30B	E.E. DB1. Form K3	28 0	27 0	16 0	6 6	5 6	6 0	6 7	9 4½	(e, k)
—	1900	Works	—	—	—	?	?	?	?	?	?	?	—	?	—	—	—	—	Nothing known.

(b) Second-hand Cars.

Car Numbers	Date Built	Type of car	Seating In	Seating Out	Side windows	Body builder	Truck	Wheel Base	Motors	Type of Controller	Length: Overall	Over Dashes	Over Corner Pillars	Width: Overall	Over Sills	Height: at Pillars	Lower Saloon	Trolley Plank	Notes
1–5	1913	DD.OT	23	35	4	U.E.C.	U.E.C. "Preston"	8 0	Dick Kerr DK.20	D.K. DB1. Form K3B	29 6	28 6	18 0	6 4½	6 0	6 3	6 7	9 5	(e, f) ex-W. Hartlepool, 1927.
6–7	1904	DD.CT	22	27	4	Brush	B & M "Tividale"	8 6	?	?	27 0	26 0	16 0	6 3	5 8	6 0	6 7	16 0	(e) ex-Birmingham & Midland 1930.

No.	Year	Type				Body	Truck			Motor		Control																		Notes
8–9	1913	DD.CT	22	34	3	U.E.C.	U.E.C. "Preston"	8	0	Siemens	?	Siemens	27	6	26	6	16	0	6	6	5	9	6	3	6	2	15	3½	(e, f) ex-Darlington 1926.
10	1904	DD.CT	22	27	4	Brush	B & M "Tividale"	8	6	?	?	27	0	26	0	16	0	6	3	5	8	6	0	6	7	16	0		(e) ex-Birmingham & Midland 1930.
11–12	1915	DD.CT	22	26	4	B & M Works	B & M "Tividale"	8	6	B.T-H. GE.248	?	27	0	26	0	16	0	6	3	5	8	6	0	6	7	16	0		(e, g)-do-1928.
14	1913	DD.CT	22	26	4	B & M Works	B & M "Tividale"	8	6	?	?	27	0	26	0	16	0	6	3	5	8	6	0	6	7	16	0		(e) - do - 1930.
17	1904	DD.CT	22	27	4	Brush	B & M "Tividale"	8	6	?	?	27	0	26	0	16	0	6	3	5	8	6	0	6	7	16	0		(e) - do - 1930.
19–20	1905	DD.CT	22	27	3	U.E.C.	Brill 21.E	6	6	Dick Kerr DK.33N	D.K. S.7	27	6	26	6	16	0	6	3	5	6	6	0	6	9	16	2½	(e, f) ex-Birmingham Corporation. 1933.
21	1905	DD.CT	22	27	3	U.E.C.	Brill 21.E	6	0	Dick Kerr DK.25B	D.K. D1.G Form G1.	27	6	26	6	16	0	6	3	5	6	6	0	6	9	16	2½	(e, f) - do - 1933.
22	1905	DD.OT	22	26	3	U.E.C.	Brill 21.E	6	0	Dick Kerr DK.25B	D.K. D1.G Form G1.	27	6	26	6	16	0	6	3	5	6	6	0	6	9	9	0	(e, f, j)-do-1933.

NOTES

(a) Fitted with reversed stairs.
(b) With twin sliding doors to saloon.
(c) With Clerestory roof.
(d) Thanet Nos. 21–40 as rebuilt.
(e) With single sliding door to saloon.
(f) With vestibuled platforms.
(g) With partial vestibules to platforms.
(h) Dover Nos. 13, 15 & 16 rebuilt with full canopies (13 & 16 vestibuled).
(j) Top cover removed and upper deck fittings from old No. 22 substituted.
(k) Ex-B & M top covers fitted in 1928.
(l) Nos. 3 & 10 originally not motored and used as trailers.
DD — Double deck.
OT — Open Top.
CT — Covered Top.
Works — Works or service car.
* Thanet No. 40 rebuilt again in 1927 with 4 windows and Peckham 6ft. 6in. truck.
For full names of manufacturers see chapters concerned.

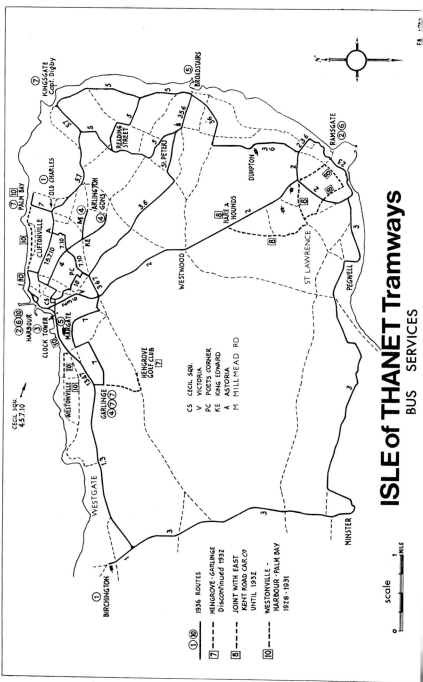

ISLE of THANET Tramways

BUS SERVICES

CS CECIL SQU.
V   VICTORIA
PC POETS CORNER
KE KING EDWARD
A   ASTORIA
M   MILLMEAD RD

① ⑩   1936 ROUTES

⑦ ----   HENGROVE-GARLINGE
         Discontinued 1932

⑧ ----   JOINT WITH EAST
         KENT ROAD CAR Cº
         UNTIL 1932

⑩ ----   WESTONVILLE -
         HARBOUR - PALM BAY
         1928 - 1931

scale
0 _____ 1 MILE

FR 1792

356

Motor Bus Services operated by

ISLE OF THANET ELECTRIC SUPPLY COMPANY

Route 1.	1928 — Margate Harbour — Westgate — Birchington Station.		Every hour.
	1931 — ,, ,, ,, ,, ,,		Every 30 minutes.
	1932 — ,, ,, ,, ,, ,,		Every 20 minutes.
	1936 — "Old Charles" — Margate Harbour — Westgate — Birchington Station.		Every 20 minutes.
	1937 — Replaced by East Kent route 51. Margate Harbour — Westgate only.		
Route 2.	1928 — Margate Harbour — Westwood — Ramsgate Harbour (loop).		Every hour.
	1931 — ,, ,, ,, ,, ,, ,,		Every 30 minutes.
	1932 — ,, ,, ,, ,, ,, ,,		Every 20 minutes.
	1936 — ,, ,, ,, ,, ,, ,,		,, ,, ,,
	1937 — Replaced by East Kent route 52.		
Route 3.	"Thanet Circular".		
	1928 — Margate—Westgate—Birchington—Minster—Pegwell Bay—Ramsgate —Broadstairs—St. Peters—Victoria Inn—Margate.		Every hour approx.
	1931 — as above.		Every 30 minutes
	1932 — as above, but slight diversion in Ramsgate.		,, ,, ,,
	1936 — as above.		,, ,, ,,
	1937 — Replaced by East Kent route 56.		
Route 4.	1928 — Garlinge—Margate Station—Cecil Square—"King Edward".		Every 15 minutes.
	1931 — Garlinge—Margate Station—Cecil Square—Dane Valley. (alternate journeys to Mill Mead Road or Arlington Gdns.)		,, ,, ,,
	1932 & 1936 — as above.		,, ,, ,,
	1937 — Replaced by East Kent route 54 to Mill Mead Road. 54A to Arlington Gardens.		
Route 5.	1928 Margate Station—Cliftonville—Kingsgate—Reading Street—St. Peters— Broadstairs (two loops used by alternate journeys).		Every 10 minutes.
	1931 — as above, some journeys start from Garlinge.		,, ,, ,,
	1932 & 1936 as 1928.		,, ,, ,,
	1937 — Replaced by East Kent routes 55, 55A & 55B.		
Route 6.	1928 — Margate Harbour—St. Peters—Broadstairs—Dumpton—Ramsgate Harbour.		Irregular.
	1931–1936 as above.		Every 90 minutes.
	1937 — Replaced by East Kent route 53.		
Route 7.	1928 — Palm Bay—Paladium Garage—Margate Station—Garlinge. (certain journeys extended to Hengrove Golf Course).		Every 75 minutes.
	1931 — as 1928.		,, ,, ,,
	1932 & 1936 — as above, but Hengrove journeys withdrawn.		Every hour.
	1937 — Replaced by East Kent route 57 Garlinge—Margate—Garlinge (circular).		
Route 8.	"Ramsgate Town Service" (Joint with East Kent).		
	1928 — Newington "Hare & Hounds"—St. Lawrence—Ramsgate Town Stn. —King Street (loop).		Every 20 minutes.
	1931 — as above.		,, ,, ,,
	1932 — Replaced by East Kent route later numbered 72. (Thanet not participating).		
Route 9.	No Thanet route carried this number between 1928 and 1937.		
Route 10.	1928 — Palm Bay—Cliftonville—Margate Harbour—Westonville—Westgate Bay Avenue.		Every hour.
	1931 — as above.		Every 30 minutes.
	1932 — Service discontinued.		
	1936 — "Margate Town Circular". Margate Harbour—Cecil Square—Cliftonville—"Astoria"— Margate Harbour.		Every 40 minutes.
	1937 — Replaced by East Kent route 63.		
Tram Route.	"Main Line".		
	1928 to 1936 — Westbrook—Margate Harbour—Cliftonville—St. Peters— Broadstairs Front—Ramsgate Harbour—St. Lawrence—Ramsgate Town Station.		Every few minutes.
	1937 — Replaced by East Kent routes 49 & 49A, starting from Birchington Stn. (opposite ways round loop in Ramsgate—49 via Crescent Rd. & Paragon. 49A via Grange Rd. & St. Augustine's Road).		
	"Top Road".		
	1928 to 1936 — Broadstairs Station—Salisbury Avenue—Ramsgate Harbour.		Every Hour.
	1937 — Service withdrawn and not replaced.		

NOTE. The list above is based on Thanet Company's timetables for 1928, 1931, 1932 and 1936, kindly loaned by D.H.D. Spray.
The double deck buses normally worked on route 2.

---

173. Opposite—Map of motor bus services operated by the Thanet Company in the 1920s & 1930s.
E. Beddard.

ISLE OF THANET ELECTRIC SUPPLY COMPANY LIMITED
Motor Bus Fleet

(a) Original Fleet (1913 to early 1920s).

Fleet No.	Registration Number	Make	Type	Seating	Chassis No.	Date	East Kent No.	Remarks
1.	R.17	Straker Squire	S.D.	14	—	1913	—	Withdrawn 1920/21.
2.	?	Dennis	,,	14	—	1913	—	,, ,,
3.	FR.1923?	Tilling Stevens TS.3A	,,	20	—	?	—	Became No.' 1.
4.	?	Leyland	S.D.	26	—	?	—	Withdrawn 1920/21.
5.	KT.4648?	Straker Squire	,,	?	—	1915	—	Converted to lorry.
6.	KN.3519	Thornycroft "J"	O.T.	50	7191	1919	—	Renumbered 2.
7.	KT.8095?	Straker Squire	S.D.	?	—	1916	—	Converted to lorry.
8.	?	?	?	?	—	?	—	Not Known.
9.	LF.8832	L.G.O.C. "B"	O.T.	34	2221	acq. 1921	—	ex-West Margate Co.
10.	LH.8277	,, ,,	,,	?	3474	,, ,,	—	,, ,, ,,
11.	KE.4726	A.E.C. ,,	S.D.	?	?	,,	—	,, ,, ,,
12.	KE.7766	?	,,	,,	?	,,	—	,, ,, ,,
15.		See No. 11 renumbered.						
16.		See No. 12 renumbered.						
17.	KM.7766	Berliet	S.D.	20	?	acq. 1926	—	ex-Carlton Coaches.
18.	KM.1918	,,	,,	,,	?	,, ,,	—	,, ,,
								(Became lorries C & E)
—	KN.9723	Tilling Stevens	,,	?	?	,, 1924	—	Second Hand ?

(b) Fleet of the 1920s

Fleet No.	Registration Number	Make	Type	Seating	Chassis No.	Date	East Kent No.	Remarks
1.	FR.1923	Tilling Stevens	S.D.	20	?	?	—	Old No. 3
2.	KN.3519	Thornycroft "J"	O.T.	50	7191	1919	—	Scrapped 1926.
3.	KN.2568	,, ,,	,,	,,	7242*	,,	—	,, ,,
4.	KN.3071	,, ,,	,,	,,	7244*	,,	—	,, ,,
5.	KN.2859	,, ,,	,,	,,	7164	,,	—	,, ,,
6.		Renumbered 2 which see above.						
7.	?	?	?	?	?	?	—	Not known.
8 or 10.	KL.6153	Thornycroft "A2"	S.D. n/c	20	11508	1925	—	Scrapped ?
9.	KL.6154	,, ,,	,, ,,	,,	11509	,,	—	,,
10.		See No. 8 above.						
11.	KL.6672	Thornycroft "A2"	,, ,,	,,	11328	1926	1049	To East Kent 1937
12.	KL.6673	,, ,,	,, ,,	,,	11327	,,	1054	,, ,,
13.	KM.3171	,, ,,	,, ,,	,,	12776	,,	1042	,, ,,
14.	KM.3172	,, ,,	,, ,,	,,	12777	,,	1043	,, ,,
15.	KO.9819	,, "BC"	S.D. f/c	32	16274	1928	1055	,, ,,
16.	KO.9818	,, ,,	,, ,,	,,	16273	,,	1056	,, ,,
17.	KM.7766	Berliet	Lorry	,,	—	1926	—	Became Lorry "C".
18.	KM.1918	,,	,,	,,	—	1926	—	Became Lorry "E".
19.	KM.5628	Thornycroft "A2"	S.D. n/c	20	12801	1926	1049	To East Kent 1937.
20.	KM.5627	,, ,,	,, ,,	,,	12800	,,	1048	,, ,,
21.	KM.5834	Berliet	—	30	—	1926	—	ex-Carlton Coaches Converted to lorry
22.	KM.5626	Thornycroft "A2"	S.D. f/c	20	12799	1926	1047	To East Kent 1937
23.	KM.5625	,, ,,	,, ,,	,,	12798	,,	1046	,, ,,
24.	KO.2780	,, "BC"	,, ,,	30	13479	1927	—	Converted to lorry
25.	KO.2779	,, ,,	,, ,,	,,	13478	,,	—	,, ,, ,,
26.	KP.419	,, ,,	O.T.	48	16276	1928	1039	To East Kent 1937
27.	KP.418	,, ,,	,, ,,	,,	16275	,,	1038	,, ,,
28.	KP.7816	Daimler "CF.6"	S.D. n/c	30	7223	1929	1052	,, ,,
29.	KP.7815	,, ,,	,, ,,	,,	7221	,,	1051	,, ,,
30.	KP.7817	,, ,,	,, ,,	,,	7225	,,	1053	,, ,,
31.	KP.7818	,, ,,	,, ,,	,,	7227	,,	—	Not renumbered by EK
32.	KR.4714	,, ,,	,, ,,	,,	7321	,,	1044	To East Kent
33.	KR.4715	,, ,,	,, ,,	,,	7323	,,	1045	,, ,, 1937
34.	KR.5086	,, ,,	O.T. f/c	48	7400	,,	1041	,, ,, ,,
35.	KR.5085	,, ,,	,, ,,	,,	7408	,,	1040	,, ,, ,,
36.	VA.9868	,, ,,	S.D. f/c	32	7808	1930	1057	ex-Lanarkshire Tr.Co.
37.	VA.9892	,, ,,	,, ,,	,,	7884	,,	1068	,, ,,
38.	VA.9896	,, ,,	,, ,,	,,	7834	,,	1072	,, ,,
39.	VA.9899	,, ,,	,, ,,	,,	7886	,,	—	,, Not to EK.
40.	VA.9877	,, ,,	,, ,,	,,	7830	,,	1059	,, ,,

Note. — S.D.—Single deck.   n/c="Normal control" i.e. driver behind engine.
  f/c—"Forward control" i.e. driver beside engine.   O.T.=Open top.   C.T.=covered top.
  *— Ex-War Dept. chassis with open top bodies ex old Nos. 9 & 10 lengthened to 50 seats.

Fleet No.	Registration No.	Make		Type	Seating	Chassis No.	Date	East Kent No.	Remarks
41.	VA.9890	Daimler	"CF.6"	S.D. f/c	32	7852	,,	1067	*Ex-Lanarkshire Tr.Co.*
42.	VA.9882	,,	,,	,, ,,	,,	7838	,,	1061	,, ,,
43.	VA.9886	,,	,,	,, ,,	,,	7836	,,	1064	,, ,,
44.	VA.9893	,,	,,	,, ,,	,,	7850	,,	1069	,, ,,
45.	VA.9895	,,	,,	,, ,,	,,	7870	,,	1071	,, ,,
46.	VA.9900	,,	,,	,, ,,	,,	7856	,,	1079	,, ,,
47.	VA.9915	,,	,,	,, ,,	,,	7888	,,	1078	,, ,,
48.	KV.103	,,	"CH.6"	C.T. f/c	48	9065	?	1031	ex-Demonstrator.
49.	FS.3388	,,	"CP.6"	,, ,,	51	9107	?	1037	ex-Edinburgh ?.
50.	ADU.470	,,	"COG.5"	,, ,,	56	9223	?	1032	Later renumbered 1.
51.	CKP.876	,,				9713	?	1033	Later renumbered 2.
52.	VA.9888	,,	"CF.6"	S.D. f/c	32	7862	1930	1066	ex-Lanarkshire Tr.Co.
53.	VA.9885	,,	,	,, ,,	,,	7846	,,	1063	,, ,,
54.	VA.9914	,,	,,	,, ,,	,,	7872	,,	1077	,, ,,
55.	VA.9908	,,	,,	,, ,,	,,	7868	,,	1074	,, ,,
56.	VA.9887	,,	,,	,, ,,	,,	7848	,,	1065	,, ,,
*57 ?	VA.9877 or VA.9894	,,	,,	,, ,,	,,	7828 or 7850	,,	1060 1070	,, ,, ,, ,,
58.	VA.9909	,,	,,	,, ,,	,,	7876	,,	1075	,, ,,
59.	VA.9871	,,	,,	,, ,,	,,	7810	,,	1057	,, ,,
60.	VA.9911	,,	,,	,, ,,	,,	7878	,,	1076	,, ,,
61.	VA.9906	,,	,,	,, ,,	,,	7842	,,	1073	,, ,,
62.	VA.9884	,,	,,	,, ,,	,,	7860	,,	1062	,, ,,

(c) Replacements in the 1930s.

1.	ADU.470	Daimler	"COG.5"	C.T. f/c	56	9223	?	1032	Formerly No. 50.
2.	CKP.876	,,	,,	,, ,,	,,	9713	,,	1033	Formerly No. 51.
3.	CKP.877	,,	,,	,, ,,	,,	9714	1936	1034	To East Kent 1937.
4.	CKP.878	,,	,,	,, ,,	,,	9715	,,	1035	,, ,,
5.	CKP.879	,,	,	,, ,,	,,	9716	,,	1036	,, ,,

Note. Two ex-Lanarkshire buses had not yet received Thanet numbers, when taken over by E.K.

Overleaf — **SOME TYPICAL BUSES IN THE THANET FLEET**

174. Upper—Thornycroft BC type open topper No. 26 of 1928.
175. Middle Thornycroft A2 type one man bus No. 20 of 1926, with ex-Lanarkshire Daimler No. 58 behind.
176. Lower—The last word — Daimler COG type No. 4 of 1936.

All three photos by D. W. K. Jones.

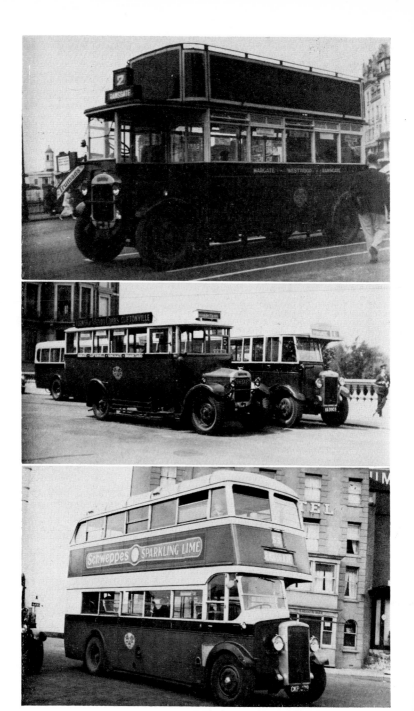

360